D&T
CHALLENGES

DESIGN & TECHNOLOGY 11-14

A CTC Trust programme sponsored and
supported by the Royal College of Art,
the Esmée Fairbairn Trust and the
Department for Education

Hodder & Stoughton

A MEMBER OF THE HODDER HEADLINE GROUP

Acknowledgements

The publishers would like to thank the following:

Danny Jenkins of fab 4 studio for the cover illustration; Lynda King for the cover and book design; Tim Perry for illustrations on pp 99–103; Ann Baum, Peter Dennis, Pauline King, Sally Launder, Isobel Morgan-Giles, Tony Morris, Gary Rees, Jacqui Thomas and Lorna Turpin of **Linda Rogers Associates** for the illustrations.

We are grateful to the following companies agencies and individuals who have given permission to reproduce photographs in this book. Every effort has been made to trace and acknowledge ownership of copyright. The publishers will be glad to make suitable arrangements with any copyright holder whom it has not been possible to contact

J. Allan Cash (12 left, 14 top right, 20, 21 top left, 21 top centre, centre right, 50 left, 60, 68 bottom top right, 78 top right, 112 middle right (both) and bottom); Andrew Ross Photography (10, 14); Arvid/Barry Jones (47); Badal/Oxfam (16, 18); G.I. Bernard (68 bottom left); John Birdsall Photography (6, 8, 32 both, 37 top left, top right, middle left, bottom right, 39 bottom left, 45 top, 51 all 3, 77 all); Bernard Brandham (12 centre middle, 13 top, 14 top centre); Brother Ltd (22 bottom middle); Dr Jeremy Burgess/Science Photo Library (61); Christies Images (72 bottom, 74 top right, bottom, 73, 75 top); Colourific (84 both); Bill Coward (66 top); Chris Davies (27 both, 31, 40, 41, 44, 45 bottom, 48, 99, 105 bottom left, top right and bottom right, 107 all three, 108 both); Dennis Publishing (33); Dexion (87 top); Dover Publications Ltd (75); Mary Evans Picture Library (113 bottom right); Embroiderer's Guild (16, 17); Express Newspapers (69); Fine Colour Packaging (80 both); Ford (97 left and right); Froud/Jim Pascoe (19); Ginsters/Trevor G. Burrows (52, 53, 58); Globe Theatre (19 top right); Gourmet Chocolates Ltd (7, 11); David Guyon, The BOC Group PLC/Science Photo Library (60); Robert Harding Picture Library (14 left, 21 bottom left, 22 bottom left, 39 top left, 74 top left); Hulton Picture Library (37 left and bottom left); Hutchinson Library (12 top, middle right, bottom, 21 middle centre, 39 middle right, 78 left, bottom right, middle left, 22 top right, centre); Hutchinson Library/R.I. Lloyd (14 centre); Jacqui Hurst (21 top right, 22 bottom right, 39 top right); Richard Kirby/Oxford Scientific Films Ltd (62); Caroline Lucas/Oxfam (39 bottom right); Dick Luria/Science Photo Library (63); Maclaren (98 top); Marks and Spencer Plc. (41, 43, 104 both); Jerry Mason/New Scientist/Science Photo Library (84 top right); John Murray (35); Nancy Durrel Mckenna (78 middle); National Motor Museum, Beaulieu (66); Pashley (96 left); Photo Library International/Science Photo Library (76 left); Portsmouth City Council (18); Lisa Prescott, Exeter St. Thomas High School, Devon (105 top left); Product First Ltd. (121 both, 122 all three); Mary Quant (113 top right); Queensbury Hunt (87 bottom); Billie Rafaeli and Ben Edwards (88, 98, 112, top left bottom left and top right, 113 all left); Raleigh (94, 95, 96 right); Rex/John Shelley (114); Andrew Ross Photography (10, 14, 100, 101); Rover Ltd. (76 right); Brian Russell/Dixons CTC (68 top left, 71); Shell mileage marathon (67); The Illustrated London News Picture Library (72); Victoria and Albert Museum (13 bottom); Weidenfeld and Nicholson (39 top middle); Westland Helicopters (46, 49 both); World Crafts/Oxfam (18, 19 both, 22 top left).

Cataloguing in Publication Data is available from the British Library

ISBN 0 340 63927 X

First published 1995

Impression number	10	9	8	7	6	5	4	3	2	1
Year	1998		1997		1996		1995			

Typeset by Wearset, Boldon, Tyne and Wear.
Printed in Great Britain for Hodder & Stoughton Educational, a division of Hodder Headline Plc, 338 Euston Road, London NW1 3BH by Cambus Litho Ltd, East Kilbride

ROYAL COLLEGE OF ART SCHOOLS TECHNOLOGY PROJECT

The Royal College of Art Schools Technology Project is a three year programme which started in September 1993. It is designed to raise the sights and cater for the curricular needs of technology teachers in secondary schools. The project is funded by the Esmée Fairbairn Charitable Trust, Cable and Wireless plc and the Department for Education.

The underlying purpose is to improve the quality of technology education throughout secondary schools in England.

The Project's central team is based at the Royal College of Art, supporting developments in 13 selected secondary schools with Teacher Fellows on part-time secondment. They are developing a comprehensive design and technology course for students aged 11 to 19. The whole team is working closely with business organisations and major industrial companies to ensure a curriculum which is relevant to the worlds of business and commerce.

This student book forms part of the course developed to deliver the requirements of, and enhance the National Curriculum and post-14 work, particularly for GNVQ.

Royal College of Art Schools Technology Project – Writing team

Teacher Fellows and partner schools

Alan Booth (Wymondham College, Norfolk)
Claire Buxton (Islington Sixth Form Centre, London)
Anne Constable (Beauchamp College, Leicester)
Corinne Harper (Burntwood School for Girls, London)
Dai James (Ashfield School, Nottinghamshire)
Mary Moran (Kingsway School, Cheadle)
Barbara Mottershead (Shevington High School, Wigan)
Robin Pellatt (Bishop David Brown School, Woking)
Rob Petrie (Exeter St Thomas High School, Devon)

Richard Pinnock (Vale of Catmose School, Rutland)
Mark Rogers (Brooke Weston CTC, Northants)
Brian Russell (Dixons CTC, Bradford)
Kalvin Turner (Bosworth Community College, Leicester)

Project team

David Perry, Project Director
Louise T Davies, Assistant Project Director
Alan Wheelhouse, Assistant Project Director
Maria Kyriacou, Project Assistant

Acknowledgements

Our special thanks to all of the Teacher Fellows and their schools and particularly their colleagues, partners, friends and children who supported them, whilst they were writing to meet the deadlines.

The Royal College of Art Schools Technology Project wishes to extend its thanks to the following for their support and help in the writing of this book: Kathleen Lund (Chief Executive) and her colleagues at the CTC Trust, the Department for Education, Office for Standards in Education (OFSTED), the Royal College of Art, and their representatives on the Project Management Group; Joanne Catmull (Marks and Spencer plc), Graham Cornish (Ginsters Ltd), Dorothy Tucker (Embroiderers' Guild), Talitha Blythe-Lord, Gill Fine and Stephanie Valentine (British Nutrition Foundation), Julie Plenty (Department of Health), Robert Glassup (Gourmet Chocolates Ltd), Michael Diesendorff (Husqvarna Viking), Nick Swift (Economatics), Jed Gisborne and Chris Quigley (Fine Colour Packaging), Westland Aerospace, Farnell Electronics, Derek Kendall (Metal Box), Derek Waeland (McLaren Cars), David Barnard and Steve Conway (Denfords Machine Tools), Product First, Julie Speers and Alan Youngman (Kemnal Technology College), John Lloyd (Mosely Park School), David Lathan (Kingshurst CTC), Sue Harvey and Sarah Wilberforce (Burntwood School), Russell Fisher (Bosworth College), Kath Twist (Shevington High School).

And finally, thanks to Catherine Boulton at Hodder & Stoughton for her enthusiasm in keeping up the team spirit!

Contents

Designing and making – the challenges

This book challenges you to come up with original ideas, to develop them into exciting designs and to make your designs really well. We challenge you to understand the technologies available to us, and to question how they are used.

If you do, you will come to enjoy the world of design and technology. You will take part in one of the most satisfying and necessary activities of humankind – making the world a better place for us to live in.

Design is challenging – designing is a difficult business. Any of us can criticise the buildings and products we meet in our lives. There is no ideal way of designing anything – what's best for one person is rarely best for another. You might want one thing from a product and I might want something else. So you need to learn how to consider other people's needs and to design for them – not just yourself. You need to learn too what's most important in your design. But there are some challenges here which should produce for you some satisfying additions to your life.

This book contains twelve activities, each of which starts with a design challenge.

Your challenge

In this area of the page you will find an introduction to the challenge and some of the background information you need to understand it. There are some pictures with it which you should look at carefully because they are there to help you. They give more information and suggest some ideas if you study them closely. Ask questions about the pictures: What is this? Why is it here? How can this help me?

At this stage of your course your teachers will do a lot of the planning for you, or with you. But if you always try to look ahead, and sometimes to look back, you will understand better how to do the planning yourself and organise your projects successfully.

Why this activity is useful

Unless you understand why an activity is in your course, we cannot expect you to be committed to it. Every project has been planned for good reason. Each one helps you to learn good designing and making skills. Some of these skills are shown in this part of the page.

Designing and making – the challenges

Sometimes there is information about an industrial project which relates to your challenge. There are people working in the adult world on similar designing and making activities to all those in this book. We hope you will want to find our more about the examples we give.

The broader picture . . .

Each challenge provokes important questions. Many of them question our values – things that are important to us personally. In this box we offer you some start-off questions. Your teacher may suggest you answer these on your own or in discussions. If not, think about them yourself and see what answers you come up with.

But be warned – they're not easy!

To be successful

Before you start on any challenge you need to understand what you need to do to succeed. These lists tell you how you should work on the assignment, and what is important in it. They will guide your evaluation and sometimes assessment.

Check them from time to time as you work to make sure you are on the right track

Planning things through

You will have realised by now that we want you to learn to take more and more responsibility. Only by learning this can you become a responsible adult. We do not believe that you should depend on your teacher to plan everything for you.

Ready, Steady, Go!

What will the design and technology challenges be like?

Some projects will be short, others will be longer. Over the year you will make more choices and begin to manage your own projects. Sometimes your teachers will tell you what to do. They will start you off and lead the challenge by giving you tasks to do. This will help you to learn the skills and knowledge you need to design and make things. You can do some tasks at home or in your own time. Your teacher may:

◆ get you to work on your own
◆ get you to work in a group
◆ get you to work with a partner
◆ give different tasks to different people.

You will be:
◆ finding information
◆ getting ideas by trying things out
◆ looking at other products
◆ creating your own ideas
◆ developing them into well thought out designs
◆ making them
◆ testing how well they work
◆ thinking about how well you are doing in design and technology.

You may not always be working on the same thing as the other students in your class. If you finish your challenge your teacher may give you another exciting task to follow, before the whole class starts on the next challenge.

What can I do already?

You've been doing design and technology for six school years! What have you enjoyed doing in design and technology? Have a look through this book and discuss with a partner what you have learned already which will help you with the tasks.

You could bring in a piece of **design** and **technology** work that you have done before and that you are proud of to show the class. How did you make it?

Getting ready for work

You will be working with **equipment** and in rooms where there are strict rules for your own **safety** and the safety of your friends. You will know some of the rules from your previous work, but the beginning of this new school year is a good time to remind yourself how important safety is. You should take responsibility for safety – your teacher is relying on you.

Safety rules
1 Be sensible. Do not rush about.
2 Work tidily. Put things away in the right place.
3 Carry sharp tools and hot items very carefully.
4 Use the right tools for the job.
5 Wear the right safety gear, including goggles, masks and hairnets.
6 Never distract someone at a machine.

What am I going to learn this year?

There are 12 challenges in this book and your teacher will pick a course made up of those which are the best for your class. You are unlikely to do them all this year! All the challenges ask you to design and make things. You will use all sorts of different **materials** and **components**, including food, textiles, plastics, wood, metal and electronics. Sometimes you will work with two materials together – have a look at the *Puppets* or *Novelty chocolates* challenges as examples of this.

Design and Technology should be fun – it's about doing things rather than just writing and reading.

Over this year you will improve the quality of the products you design and make. Your work will get better and more complex. Throughout this book you will find examples

Case Studies

of designing and making from the adult world. During your school years your aim is to improve your work until it becomes more like these examples.

Who helps me in Design and Technology?

There are lots of people who can help you with your designing and making. They include teachers, technicians, librarians, your schoolmates, experts from industry, people in the community, your friends and family – and YOU.

Think for yourself. Remember YOU are an important **resource** too – you do not need to ask your teacher everything.

It is important to use resources which can help you such as . . .

'I need to .... Who will I go to? Where will I find help?'

SHOPS
NEWSPAPERS & MAGAZINES
VISITS
I.T. NETWORKS
CHALLENGE
LIBRARY

I'm stuck with this design

I don't know how to use this machine.

I need to find out about Aztecs.

These resources may not always be in the technology classrooms.

Somewhere to keep my work

Your teacher will give you something to keep your work in. It may be a folder, a folio, a book, or a box. You will have to label it clearly, keep it safe and present it attractively.

Keep your notes, sketches of your ideas, samples, tests and plans neat and tidy. Keep everything flat and clean.

Tools and machines

Here are some groups of **tools** that you will use in design and technology.
What tools do you know already? Draw and name as many tools as you can in the following groups.
Find out where these are kept in the technology classrooms.

For cutting

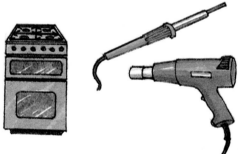

For heating

For shaping and moulding

For joining things

For holding things

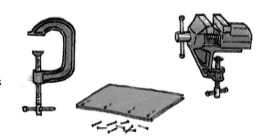

Chocoholics

Your challenge!

A chocolate factory makes chocolate **souvenirs** to give away at special events or occasions or to promote companies. It often produces **sets** for people to collect (for example, three different cars).

Focusing on one event, occasion or company **your challenge** is to design and make a shaped chocolate **novelty** in appropriate packaging.

Why this activity is useful

◆ You will find out about how chocolate is produced and about the **properties** of materials.

◆ You will learn how you have to design according to what the material will or will not do.

◆ You will also link Design and Technology work across more than one area to produce the **mould** and the chocolate.

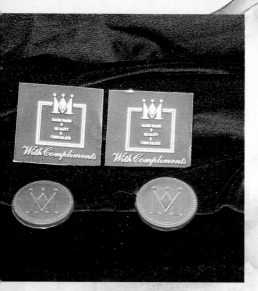

Gourmet Chocolates Ltd make chocolate novelties for a wide range of clients including hotels and companies

The broader picture . . .

Many companies produce free gifts that they give away.

◆ Try making a list of free gifts and think about why they are given away.

◆ Are the gifts free? Who pays for them?

◆ Why do companies produce sets of gifts to collect?

◆ Is it fair that companies should do this?

To be successful

★ You must be able to say *why* you chose your event or company.

★ Select a suitable design for it from a number of ideas.

★ Draw your final design accurately and make the mould precisely.

★ Choose a type of chocolate and melt it carefully so that it gives you the best result for your design – the quality of your novelty is important.

★ Create a package which will both protect the chocolate well and display it attractively.

Planning things through

Useful tips

▶ You may be able to save time by designing the shape of your novelty in your own time.

▶ Think carefully about the shape of chocolate products and which ones have most chocolate for their size.

▶ Work out how you can put features on the shape.

▶ Create a **bubble pack** from your clear mould. Use it with a backing card as a quick way to make a package.

When you finish your chocolate novelty there are other interesting tasks your teacher may let you try before the whole class begins the next challenge.

11

Ideas for your chocolate novelty

A designer always thinks about the people who will use the product.

Make a list of different events, occasions or companies. Do any of them have a theme (for example, an obvious theme for British Telecom would be telephones)?

If you've listed events, what do you think the people at them would like? If you listed companies, what would people who use your companies like?

You're going to be designing and making a small chocolate novelty for a special event or occasion or to promote a company.

Choose an event or a company. Who will be at the event? What are you promoting? List and sketch a set of shapes that you could make out of chocolate for your event or company.

Product evaluation: testing chocolate novelties

Find out about chocolate novelties you can buy already, and test them. This could be fun! (It is known as **product evaluation**). Doing this will give you ideas for your own design. You may want to sketch the products, find out how the chocolate's shape and packaging are made, and to taste the chocolate.

Designing skills: Looking at existing products 94

Where does chocolate come from?

Columbus brought the cocoa bean to Europe from Central America. Most cocoa beans now come from West Africa from trees which can grow up to 70 metres high! Cocoa pods measure 15 to 20 cm long and weigh about 0.5 kg.

Cocoa tree, pod and beans

Cocoa beans are made into chocolate. The word 'chocolate' comes from the Aztec word for 'bitter water', since without sweetener the original cocoa drink was very bitter.

Find out how chocolate is made and which chocolate will be the best for your novelty.

Using a template

1. Make a tracing of a photograph or accurate drawing of the shape you want to cut out.

2. Cut out the tracing. This is your **template**.

3. Stick your template onto a piece of **balsa wood**.

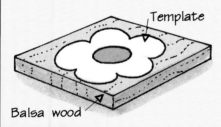

Template

Balsa wood

4. Using a **Vibrasaw** or **coping saw**, cut out the shape in the balsa wood. Your teacher will show you how to use a Vibrasaw safely, but remember to use a protective eye covering such as goggles and to hold the work securely. Smooth the edges of your shape with sandpaper.

5. If you want to add special raised features, cut out the shapes in thin card and stick them to the surface of your shape.

6. Your **former** or **plug** is now ready for you to use it on the **vacuum forming machine**. Your teacher will show you how to produce a vacuum-formed mould for your chocolate.

Casting

Casting is pouring a liquid into a mould. When the liquid sets or hardens it keeps the **form** (3-D shape) of the mould.

What materials are used for casting?

Designing skills: Thinking about production 109

Casting chocolate

Cut the chocolate into small pieces, heat it gently until it is liquid and pour it into the mould. As it cools it hardens and you can take it out of the mould.

You must use food-safe materials for your moulds

Melting chocolate

When manufacturers melt chocolate it is a carefully controlled process (called **tempering**). They have to heat the chocolate to just the right temperature, or it will be ruined.

For melting small quantities of chocolate you can use either a microwave oven or a **bain-marie**.

Melting chocolate using a bain marie

Devise a test to compare these methods and find out which one works the best.

How can you work out how much chocolate you will need to melt to fill your mould?
If you wanted to make hundreds or even thousands of your chocolate novelties how could you do it?

Did you know?

A chocolate bar helped people to invent microwave ovens.

Scientists working on radar systems for tracking down enemy aircraft during World War 2, discovered microwaves. They realised that microwave energy produced heat when a chocolate bar by a microwave emitter melted!

Bubble pack packaging

You can use the mould that you poured your chocolate into to make part of its package too.

Examples of bubble pack packaging

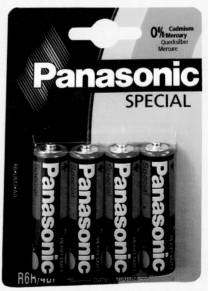

How are the chocolates that you have seen packaged?

The business of making chocolate novelties

Gourmet Chocolates Ltd design and make personalised chocolates for a range of customers. Robert Glassup (Trading Manager) tells us how they do it.

Dealing with enquiries

We never advertise our services, people hear about us by word of mouth. First of all, we discuss with a customer what they would like. We discuss the type of chocolate, the design, the packaging, the number and size of chocolates they want, and how quickly they want them delivered. We then work out how much we will charge the customer and give them a quotation.

Forming the plastic moulds

The most common mould will be a plastic sheet with 24 individual inserts. This is made using a vacuum former.

Selecting the chocolate

The chocolate used will depend a lot on the price the customer is willing to pay. We import our chocolate from Belgium and we usually get 20 tonnes at a time. The quality of the chocolate is very important. The chocolate we use has 60 per cent cocoa solids. Most bars of chocolate only contain 35 per cent cocoa solids.

Tempering

The chocolate production process begins by melting the chocolate, or 'tempering'. The chocolate is put into the tempering kettle and monitored all the time. Once it is at the right temperature and is fluid (runny) enough it is poured into the depositing machine. This injects the chocolate into each mould. The mould is vibrated to get rid of air bubbles and put in a cool room to dry.

Quality control

The chocolates are taken out of the moulds to be packed. We check that the chocolate has no air bubbles, and is the correct weight. We check that it is smooth and glossy. We snap some chocolates in half – a chocolatier (an expert in chocolate) will be able to tell if the chocolate has set well by doing this. The last inspection is to eat the chocolate. This is the best job of all!

1 Chocolate is put into the tempering kettle

2 When it is runny, it is poured into the depositing machine

3 The mould is vibrated to get rid of air bubbles

4 Then put in a cool room to dry

Why do Gourmet chocolates use a depositing machine? Would you be able to design a depositing machine to use with your mould?

Why does the company control the melting of the chocolate so carefully?

Would you be able to design a control system to monitor the temperature of your melting chocolate?

Bring a character to life

Your challenge!

Puppets and marionettes are popular with adults and children all around the world. Long before books and television were invented they were used to entertain people by acting out stories.

Puppets are fun! You can make them look amazing, ridiculous, friendly or terrifying. You can make them sing, do acrobatics, jump over mountains or turn into frogs. Puppets can make serious comments about people. Puppets are limited only by your imagination!

Your challenge is to choose or create a puppet character who interests you. It could be a person from your favourite book, a colourful god from a religious celebration, a monster, or a friendly animal which helps to teach young children about road safety.

Why this activity is useful

◆ You will learn how to emphasise the special features that give someone or something their own particular character.

◆ You will be responsible for a choice of materials. This will allow you to be creative and imaginative.

◆ This challenge will add to your knowledge of how puppets are used around the world and through the ages.

◆ You will be developing your imagination as you bring your character to life.

The broader picture . . .

Puppets are often used for satire because they exaggerate certain features (for example on *Spitting Image*). (People use satire to criticise someone or something, or to make them look ridiculous.) Sometimes this upsets or offends people.

- ◆ Does your puppet have exaggerated features?
- ◆ What are you exaggerating?
- ◆ Will your puppet upset or offend anyone?
- ◆ Does this matter? Should you change your design for this reason?
- ◆ Do you think puppets will exist in a hundred years time?

To be successful

Your puppet should be successful in two ways. It needs to be visually and functionally successful:

- ★ Try to create an interesting and unusual character – with clear, bold features which come to life when you use it.
- ★ Make sure you test your puppet out as you design and make it to be sure it will work. Make changes to make it work better if you need to.

Planning things through

Your teacher will help you to plan how to use your time for this challenge. This will help you later when you do your own planning. You might work on one part of a task and then share the information with the rest of your class before carrying on.

Understanding puppets is important to your design, so find out as much as you can about different types of puppets and how they move. Can you do this in your own time? What can you find outside school to liven up your design? Discuss with your teacher:

- ▶ What materials and equipment can you use?
- ▶ How will this affect your design?
- ▶ Is there enough time to make what you have designed? Will you need to change it?

How do puppets move?

In small groups, look at these photos and think about different kinds of puppets. What makes them move? What limits their movement?

See if you can find some real puppets to look at as well as pictures.

Rod puppet

Marionette

Glove puppet

Shadow puppet

What materials could you use?

Look at the photos on this page and make a list of all the different materials that have been used. Can you think of other materials that you could use?

Are there any materials that you will not be able to use for your puppet?

Materials you can use to make puppets

How are the puppets made?

Look carefully at one of the puppets on this page (or a real one) and describe how it has been made. Share your findings with the class.

Do you have the skills and techniques that you would need to make this puppet?

What new things might you have to learn? How will you learn them?

How can you create a character?

Who is it? A politician, pop star, film star, animal, cartoon?

How can you make its character really clear and powerful?

Can you exaggerate it?

What does 'character' mean?

What makes a successful puppet?

Finish this sentence 'A good puppet should be . . .'

Discuss this sentence with your class-mates. This will help you to work out what your puppet needs to be like to be successful.

What can you use your puppet for?

A puppet show   A play

Teaching other children

Story-telling with a book

Entertaining a young child in a car

A toy

Before you begin designing you will need to think carefully about what you want to use your puppet for.

If you were designing a puppet for a young child to use, how would this be different from designing one for a puppet show?

Team textiles

Your challenge!

Making quilts has often been an activity for a group of people working together. Sitting together working on a quilt used to be called a Sewing Bee – they are still popular in the USA.

Your class's challenge is to work in a team and to design together a wall hanging for a particular purpose. Each person will make a separate piece or section, and you will then join the sections together to create the finished wall hanging.

Your group has to agree on what the wall hanging is going to be for – it could tell a story or a legend from local history, it could be for a children's day room in a hospital, or it could tell others something about your class as a group.

Why this activity is useful

◆ You will find out what it is like to work together with your class on a joint project.

◆ You will discover the advantages of working as a team, such as sharing out the work, creating more ideas and overcoming any difficulties.

◆ By working together in this way you will be manufacturing something in the same way that people have used for many many centuries.

◆ You will also learn more about the origins of textile materials in your daily life.

The broader picture . . .

- What can you find out about 'Sewing Bees' and making items in groups?
- Why do you think this type of activity is important in communities?
- Who works at home these days?
- Do the same people work at home today as in the past?

To be successful

- You will design and make a piece or section that fits in well with the class hanging.
- Your section will be well stitched (or made) and well finished.
- You need to understand how your **fabric** was constructed.
- You will make a successful contribution to the work of the group.
- The finished hanging will do what you meant it to and please the group. The hanging can be seen clearly from a distance.

Planning things through

Your teacher will help the class to make a plan to get everything done to meet the deadline. You must complete your work on time or you will let the rest of the group down.

Check your plan each lesson to make sure you are keeping to it.

- How much time have you got as a group to spend on planning?
- How much time will you have to make your own section?
- How much time will it take to join together the final hanging?
- What skills can you bring to the group project, and what new things will you have to learn?

Designing your class wall hanging

Look at examples of wall hangings and quilts which have been made by groups of people. This will help you to think about the design of your class wall hanging.

■ What does each wall hanging tell us? What kinds of **images** or pictures are used?

■ What makes the design attractive to you? Does it make you want to get closer or be able to touch it?

■ Describe the colours, **textures** and different methods of decorating the fabric its makers used.

■ When people make different parts of something, how can they make sure that it will fit together properly? What things did they have to think about to make it look good as one piece of work?

■ How did they make the hanging?

■ How did they make sure that the hanging or quilt would last for a long time (it was **durable**)?

What makes these wall hangings and quilts successful? Make a list of the things your class will need to think about to make your own class design a success.

Designing skills:
Thinking about aesthetics 112

How people have worked together

The Overlord Embroidery

Between 1969 and 1975 in England, people made a series of 34 panels to record in needlework the invasion of Normandy in 1944 and the events which led up to it. This is known as the Overlord Embroidery. It was carried out in **appliqué**, using traditional techniques.

Toran

Mirror work, known in India as **abhala**, is a sparkling combination of small round mirrors held in place by colourful stitches. The first colourful item to greet the visitor to a Gujarati house is a **toran**, a panel which hangs over the door as a good omen.

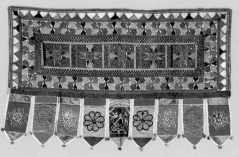

Kanthas

In Bangladesh women work collectively (together) on kanthas. Kanthas are said to represent wholeness and unity because they are made harmoniously from different parts. The art of making kanthas started as a way of quilting soft, worn out layers and patches of saris into gifts for weddings. Women work together in groups and share the image making on a quilt.

They work out of doors, their backs supported by the door post or wall of a house, with the work over their knees – a human embroidery frame!

How people have worked together (continued)

Using recycled materials

Making something beautiful out of nothing is always a challenge. Here is an example of festival decorations made from cotton scraps in India.

A message in the panel

The **arpillera** shows views of life in Latin America in stories that are passed down from mother to daughter. The women embroider together, discussing their lives, the story takes shape and they express themselves in the embroidery.

Young Embroiderers group

This hanging was made by a group of young people who belong to the Embroiderers' Guild.

Globe Theatre Project

The Globe Theatre hanging was made in New Zealand. The different parts were made separately and then assembled to complete the hanging.

Your class design

Some of the examples above show designs which are based on stories and images passed down through generations. In others the designs are based on the world around the people who made them – animals, flowers, places, people ... Their makers carefully chose patterns, colours and textures to suit the design.

What can you use to help you with your class design or your own part of the design?

Using source material to help you with ideas for your design

Designing skills: Thinking about production 109

Investigating how fabrics are made

Fibres such as cotton, wool or polyester can be **spun** or twisted into **yarns**. These yarns can then be woven, knitted or used in other ways to make fabrics.

Now look at five or six examples of fabrics. Carefully pull them apart and observe them – a magnifying glass helps. Work out how each is made.

Now **mount** each one carefully and label it to show how it is made.

Describe (by drawings and notes) the different ways fabrics are made.

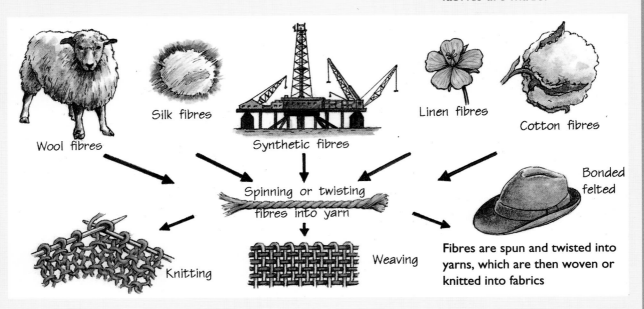

Wool fibres

Silk fibres

Synthetic fibres

Linen fibres

Cotton fibres

Spinning or twisting fibres into yarn

Knitting

Weaving

Bonded felted

Fibres are spun and twisted into yarns, which are then woven or knitted into fabrics

Is it a fibre, a yarn or a fabric?

Look at a piece of fabric. Now find in it a fibre and a piece of yarn.

Mount and label an example of a fibre, a yarn, and the fabric they came from.

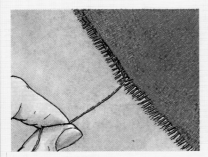

Fabric is often called '**material**' or '**textile**'- look up both these words in the dictionary.

Underneath this write a sentence showing that you understand what each word means.

Yarn (often called thread)

Fibre

Spinning

Natural fibres are short and fine so they need to be twisted into a yarn. This gives them strength so that they can be used for weaving or knitting. This twisting process is called spinning. Try spinning for yourself.

A spindle – the earliest device for twisting fibres into yarn

Investigating how fabrics are made (continued)

A spinning wheel – these were invented to make spinning less uncomfortable and to improve the yarn

A modern spinning machine – today very few people in the UK spin at home. Spinning is now done quickly and efficiently by these machines

Weaving

Many fabrics are made by weaving together two sets of threads. The threads which run down the fabric are called **warp** threads. **Weft** threads run across. Fabrics are woven on **looms**. Have a go at simple weaving.

People still use hand looms to make their fabric

A modern industrial loom – most fabric is woven on looms like these in factories around the world

Weaving can be done in different ways to create different patterns and textures in the fabrics and to give the fabrics strength, shininess, smoothness and other properties. Find out more – it is important that you understand this.

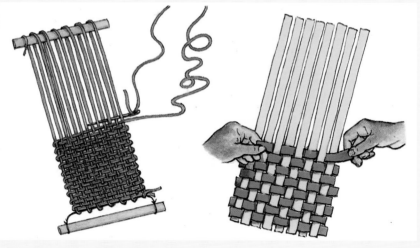

How fabric is made by weaving

Investigating how fabrics are made (continued)

Knitting

After weaving, knitting is the second most important way of making up fabrics. No one knows where knitting started.

Fabrics can be hand knitted on two or more needles, or machine knitted on hundreds of needles.

The fabric is made by creating loose knots. Knitted fabric is usually stretchy. Have a go at knitting.

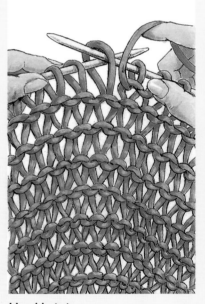

Hand knitting

Knitting machines

A range of knitted fabrics

Crochet

Crochet is still mainly done by hand. It is made using one needle or hook, but even so, it's possible to create large pieces of work. Have a go at crocheting.

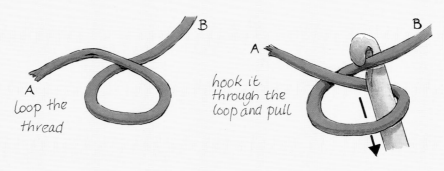

loop the thread

hook it through the loop and pull

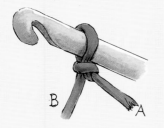

keep the loop on the hook and pull A and B tight

loop the yarn over the hook

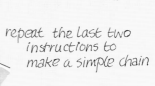

pull the yarn through the loop on the hook in the direction of the arrow

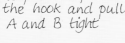

How to crochet

repeat the last two instructions to make a simple chain

Felting and bonding

Felting and **bonding** involves wetting fibres and then rolling them together. This makes them shrink and cling together to make a **mat**.

Look at something made of glass **reinforced** plastic (fibre-glass) to see if you can see the felt-like mat of glass strands. The glass is used to strengthen the plastic, which bonds it together.

Soft hats are usually made of felt – have a close look at one. Can you bring it into school to show others?

FUZZY FELT

Examples of felt, and things made from it

Private lives

Your bedroom, even if you share it, is one of the places where you can enjoy some privacy. It is nice to know that no one in your family is going to burst into your bedroom unannounced (you might be trying to do your D&T homework, or be writing secrets in your diary).

There are times, however, when the outside world needs to communicate with you.

Your challenge is to design an electrical **circuit** which warns you that someone wants to come into your room. This must be activated by a **switch** outside your bedroom.

Before anyone enters your bedroom they will press this switch, which will set off a warning buzzer inside the room.

Why this activity is useful

◆ You will learn more about electricity and making electrical circuits.

◆ You will find out about designing a product that has to fit the requirements of a particular situation.

◆ You will also need to take the views of others into account when designing and making. This is something that professional designers do all the time.

◆ You can produce your design using desk-top-publishing (**DTP**) software.

The broader picture . . .

Privacy is a very sensitive subject. Here are some points that you might like to consider:

◆ Do you think that it is important for young people to be allowed their privacy?

◆ Should your family give you some warning before coming into your bedroom?

◆ Where else do people expect privacy and need a warning that someone is going to come in?

◆ Do you disagree with any of these?

To be successful

★ If your switch is going to be a feature of your bedroom door it should grab people's attention and say something about the person that you are.

★ It should be easy for anyone to use and be visually attractive.

★ It should have a **membrane switch** that controls the buzzer system effectively.

★ You should be able to change the battery easily.

★ It should be good enough for you to want to use it at home.

Planning things through

▶ You will make the circuit that controls your door buzzer from a number of different parts called **components**. You need to plan carefully to be sure that each part of the circuit works as well as possible.

▶ You should produce a plan to show your teacher how you will do each step of this challenge.

▶ Don't forget to allow time to work out exactly where the circuit is going to go.

▶ Some of the information you need to design your circuit is given on the following pages.

Information that you will need to design your circuit

You should find out this information as part of your homework:

■ Where will you fix the switch outside your room?

■ Where will the wire run to get from the switch to the door buzzer inside your bedroom?

■ How much wire will this need?

■ Where will you attach the buzzer and battery inside your room?

■ You will find drawings (with measurements) showing all this information very useful.

Remember how electrical circuits work?

For an electrical circuit to work there must be a complete path of **conducting** material for electricity to flow round. Electricity will only flow round a circuit if a force is applied – it has to be pushed. For your bedroom

light the force comes from mains electricity. With your door buzzer this force is provided by the batteries.

If you are unsure about any of this you will need to do the electrical current refresher task which your teacher should have.

Drawing electrical circuits using symbols

The circuit that you are going to produce has different parts, called components. Some will be inside your room and others outside.

You can draw your circuit as a diagram. Designers who work with electrical or electronic

components use diagrams with special symbols to show how they are going to make a circuit.

The diagram below shows how an electrical designer might draw your door buzzer circuit.

■ Why do designers use symbols instead of pictures of the components?

■ Which would be easiest to draw?

■ Which are easiest for you to understand?

■ Which are less likely to be misunderstood?

■ Which would be easiest for a trained electrical designer to understand, if the circuit was very complex?

There is a symbol for each of the components in your circuit diagram. Make your own list of components and draw the symbol that you think represents each of them in a table. Leave spaces to add other components as you discover them later.

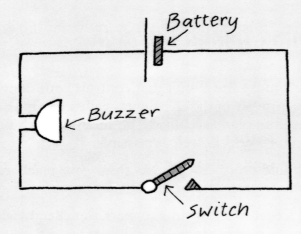

A possible door buzzer circuit

Switches for electrical circuits

One of the simplest ways of controlling whether electricity flows through your circuit or not is to use switches. A switch makes or breaks a circuit (in other words, it switches it on or off). You can also use a switch to change the direction of the flow of electricity through a circuit. A switch is one kind of **input device**.

Using switches

The easiest type of switch to use is a simple **on-off switch**.

There are many different types of switches that can be used in electrical circuits. For example if you want your switch to stay on after you let go you need a **toggle switch** (your light switches at home will be toggle switches).

Membrane switches

Membrane switches are made from thin flexible materials. They are ideal for this design situation because they can be hidden behind all sorts of front panels.

Membrane switches are used on credit card type calculators, cash registers, photocopiers and many other products.

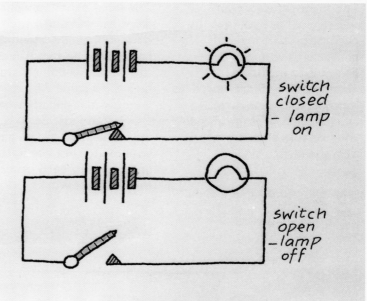

This diagram shows the switch making and breaking the circuit and so turning the lamp **on and off**.

The membrane switches in a calculator

If you want the switch to go off as soon as you let go, you need a **push-to-make switch**, such as a membrane switch.

Think what would happen if you had a toggle switch on your front door bell!

Designing your front panel

The front panel of your switch is where you put the decoration that makes it personal to you. You can design it to include a photograph or a drawing. This is called your **artwork**. Decide what part of this panel your visitors should press to turn the switch on.

Some ideas for the design of the front panel of your membrane switch.

The front panel contains the front half of your switch. The back panel will contain the back half. The two halves of the switch will be separated by a third panel with a window in it exactly where the switch must be. It is important that all the parts of your switch are accurately lined up with each other or they will not work.

If the area of the switch which your visitors press (called the window) is too big the switch will not always work properly. The switch may remain on when in fact you want it off. It is important to get the window the right size.

If you have time you could experiment to find the best size of window for your switch. If not, following these steps will help you to make a good membrane switch.

Making your switch

Before you start you should have your piece of artwork for the front panel. You also need to collect the resources you will need:

- Three pieces of card, one with a grid drawn
- Scalpel and safety rule
- Soldering iron and solder
- Adhesive copper tape
- Transparent plastic grid
- Pieces of single core wire cut to the correct lengths.

Be very accurate on all these steps or your switch will not work:

■ Decide which part of the picture on your front panel will be pressed to switch on/off. (This is called the window.)

■ Put the transparent grid over the whole frame.

■ Find the four squares that most closely cover the window area, and mark them.

■ Find the same four squares on the card grid and cut them out carefully using a scalpel and safety rule.

■ Use the window in the card to mark the position of the window on the underside of the artwork.

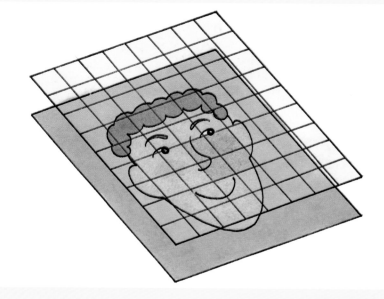

Always make sure you keep your hand clear as you hold the card

Making your switch (continued)

■ Use the window to mark (accurately again!) the position of the foil strips on the bottom piece of card.

■ Stick two strips of metal tape on to the bottom piece of card. They must go across the window but must not touch each other. (What will happen if they do?)

■ Check that you have the two lengths of **single core wire** that you need to reach from the switch outside your room to where the buzzer is going to be inside your room.

■ Carefully solder a piece of wire to the bottom of each piece of metal tape.

■ Place your piece of card with the window cut out over the bottom piece.

■ Make sure you can see both your strips of tape.

■ When you are happy with this, stick the two pieces of card together.

■ Take your artwork and stick a piece of metal tape

across the window that you have marked on the back of it.

■ Carefully stick your artwork onto the top of the card with the window.

■ Tidy the edges of your assembled switch. What ways can you think of to do this attractively?

Your switch is complete!

Output devices

When electricity is flowing round a circuit, a component which then gives out a signal (such as a buzzer giving out a sound or a lamp giving out light) is called an **output device**. An output device is a component that does something when electricity is flowing round a circuit. Your circuit could have a variety of output devices. The title of the challenge suggests a buzzer but you might want to use another output device instead, such as a lamp. If you did this though, you might need to use another sort of switch.

Finishing the circuit

When you have made your switch you can connect up and test the whole circuit by wiring your switch to a battery and a buzzer. You should test it before you solder it together, by using a **breadboard**.

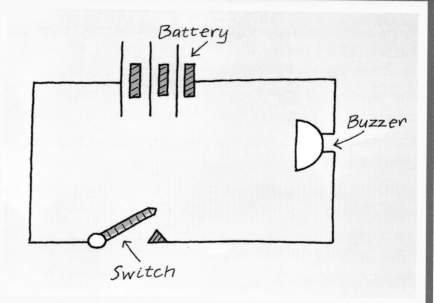

Battery

Buzzer

Switch

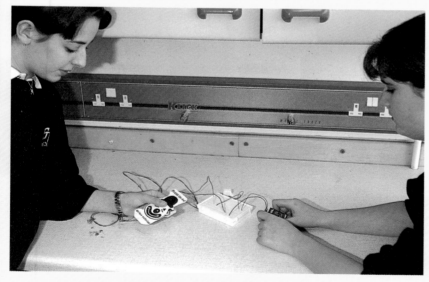

Here is a circuit diagram and a photo of a test circuit similar to the one you have made. Use them to make sure that your components are soldered together in the correct order.

These are some things you need to think about when you design the battery pack and holder:

■ How will you hold the components inside the container?

■ How will you hold the box to the artwork?

■ How will you change the battery?

■ How will the sound be allowed out of the container?

A 9 volt (PP3) battery would be best for this circuit because:

■ it will last long enough to give plenty of use

■ you can attach it to your circuit with a neat battery snap that can be soldered to your wires.

A loose battery and buzzer will look very untidy in your bedroom and will put a lot of strain on the wires. You can make your buzzer system look a lot more professional by housing your buzzer and battery together in a neat container. You could do this by vacuum-forming a holder to exactly the right size and shape.

Designing skills:
Thinking about production 109

Info pack

Your challenge!

We use computers more and more – for business and for pleasure. Many people therefore need to look after their own disks, especially in schools.

Your challenge is to design and make a means of carrying your computer disks around safely.

There are some essential features which must be included in your design:

It must be easy to carry but it must also protect the disks from damage.

It must open out to display the disks so you can find the one you want.

It should allow you to take the disks in and out freely.

It should not allow the disks to fall out accidentally.

It should carry a **logo** so that you can identify it as yours.

A student of Shevington High school displays her disk case

Why this activity is useful

You will have to choose the best materials for the job. To do this you have to think about the strength and appearance of the product. You will learn:

◆ to use a sewing machine

◆ to test and choose suitable fabrics

◆ to design and make a simple **pattern**

◆ to make a **prototype** before choosing your final idea

◆ to decorate fabric using embroidery.

You will also have made something useful which you can use.

The broader picture . . .

- ◆ What security do the disks need?
- ◆ What information about you should be kept on a computer?
- ◆ Who should be allowed to see it? What information should not be kept?
- ◆ Where could you get fabrics to re-use for your design?
- ◆ How could disk cases be made more cheaply in industry?

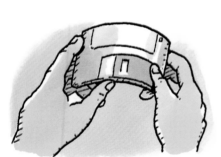

To be successful

- ★ You will investigate different materials and then choose the best one for the job.
- ★ You will work out exactly what you need to help you decide on the size, shape and construction of your disk case.
- ★ Your pattern pieces will be accurate and make a good fit.
- ★ Your machining should be neat so you have a well-finished disk case.
- ★ You will have a distinctive and original logo.
- ★ Make sure your design protects the disks as you carry them around and is easy to use. You will test your disk case by using it and evaluating how well it works.

Planning things through

For some of the tasks you will work as a team or group. This will help you to gather information more quickly – don't let your group down!

Your teacher will help you with things that you will be doing for the first time, but you will need to allow time to practise them. Can you do any of this at home?

A commercial disk case

Choosing the right material for a holder

Look at the holders in the pictures. Make a list of the properties they need, and the fabrics they are made from.

> *Designing skills:*
> Knowing what you really
> need to do → **86**

Testing fabrics to help you choose the right one

Fabric tests help you to work out which fabrics have the properties you want. Look at these examples of how some students carried out tests – they will help you to plan yours.

Here are some 'properties' words to help you:

> tough   strong   flimsy   weak   attractive   sturdy
> supportive   convenient (easy to use)   appropriate
> well-designed   well-detailed   protective (keeps it safe)
> waterproof   comfortable   stiff
> insulating (stops heat escaping)

Does it wear?

Does it stretch?

Does it resist water?

Here are some test questions:

> Does it stretch?
>
> Does it shrink?
>
> Does it wear away?
>
> Does it soak up water?
>
> Does it crease?
>
> Does it keep water out?
>
> Does it keep things warm or cool?
>
> Does it catch fire?

Generating ideas for the design of your disk case

Look back to *Your challenge!* and think about how a design could include the essential features listed there.

One way to try out some ideas is by making paper models, sticking them with sellotape or glue. This means you can try out different shapes and sizes for your disk case to see which works the best for you. It will help you to decide how you need to sew your disk case together to get the best result.

Designing skills:
Modelling   96

Making patterns and paper prototypes

Modelling a bag in paper

Use paper or card to make an accurate **prototype** of your design which you can test, and which will help you see what your holder will look like. Check that your design is the correct size and that it works. Now take your prototype to bits – the pieces are simple patterns.

Check that each piece is exactly the right size and shape. Add a 2 cm margin round each piece for the seams (this is called a **seam allowance**).

When we sew we use patterns made from paper. (They are called templates when they are used in other areas of Design and Technology.) They give you the basic shape to cut around when you are making the pieces for your disk case.

Pieces of pattern for a disk carrier. Remember that if two sides are the same we only need one pattern piece. Why?

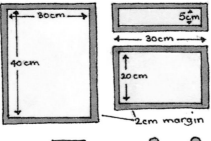

If you want one piece of fabric to have the same shape on both ends we use this method

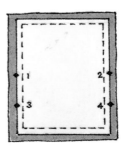

We use this symbol on the pattern so we know we have to fold the fabric in half

Sample pattern

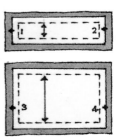

1. Sewing line
2. Cutting Line
3. Notch
4. Grain
5. Fold

Protecting the disks and reinforcing the fabric

Look at the pictures. What has been done to protect these items from damage?

Disks are sensitive and you have to look after them.

What do you need to protect your disks from?

Keep floppy disks away from magnets

Protect disks from extreme cold, heat and humidity

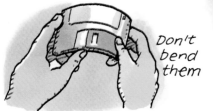

Don't bend them

Do not open disk's metal shutter.

How can you design a disk case which will do this? Will you need to reinforce the fabric that you have chosen to use? Why? To keep it stiff? To keep it flexible? To protect the edges?

Choosing and using sewing machines

There are many types of sewing machine. Some are different brands that do the same thing but look different. Others are very specialised and do one type of sewing, such as **overlocking**, or embroidering. There are computerised ones, electric ones, and manual ones. The range is huge. Look at the pictures.

As a class or in groups, find out about the types of sewing machine that are in your classroom or at home. (If you have time you could find out about other ones as well.)

Make a class chart to compare what these sewing machines can do.

Write a simple 'how to use' guide for a sewing machine. This will remind you how to set up and thread it, list important safety points, and show how to operate a sewing machine.

SEWING MACHINE	Embroidery	CAD	Overlocking	Electric
POEM	✓	✓	✗	✓
HUSQVARNA	✓	✓	✓	✓
OVERLOCKER	✗	✗	✓	✓

Joining fabric together and making the edges neat

Pieces of fabric are joined together with seams. Look at the examples

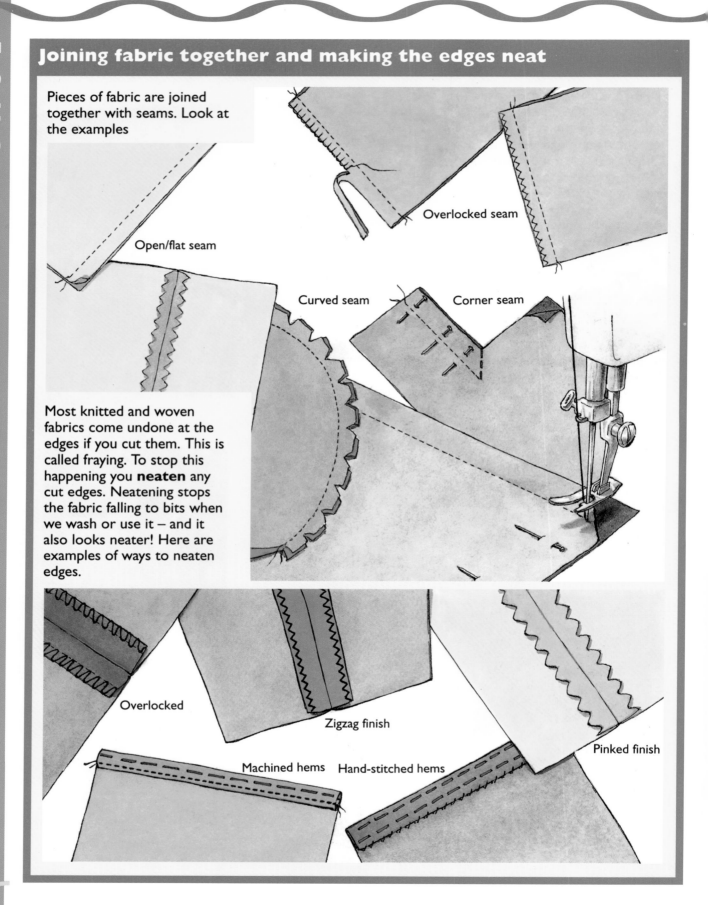

Open/flat seam

Overlocked seam

Curved seam

Corner seam

Most knitted and woven fabrics come undone at the edges if you cut them. This is called fraying. To stop this happening you **neaten** any cut edges. Neatening stops the fabric falling to bits when we wash or use it – and it also looks neater! Here are examples of ways to neaten edges.

Overlocked

Zigzag finish

Pinked finish

Machined hems   Hand-stitched hems

Personalising the outside of your disk case

Examples of embroidered bags

You can personalise the outside of your disk case with a **logo** or **motif**. Why might it be best to do this before you join the pieces of your disk case together?

Where can you get ideas for your design?

Using computer-aided designing

Using computerised sewing machines makes it easy to put a decoration on your disk case

Computerised sewing machines or embroidery machines make it easy to sew a logo or motif onto your fabric. You can draw your design on the computer screen, choose the thread colours and stitch patterns, and then transfer the logo directly onto the fabric. If you have time you can try several samples to see which one you like best before putting it onto your disk case. You can save your logo and repeat it accurately, just as manufacturers would if they were making large numbers of the same product.

Decorating fabric using embroidery

In many languages of the world, the words 'flowers', 'rivers' and 'streams' also mean embroidery. In Northern Thailand, the Lahu people are distinguished by the colour and arrangement of cloth strips sewn on to their clothes. These strips act as a striking code of identification. And as well as being decorative, the strips reinforce the openings in the clothes. Here colours, stitches and patterns are as much a part of the language as the words of a sentence.

Embroidery as decoration around the world

Healthy eating

Your challenge!

We all have our favourite foods but generally health experts recommend that we eat five helpings of fresh fruit and vegetables each day to keep our bodies healthy and working properly. *The Health of the Nation* report by the Department of Health encourages us to eat more fruit and vegetables and challenges manufacturers to develop new products which help us to do this.

Finding different ways to cook, prepare and eat fruits and vegetables is an important part of the work of a **food technologist**. Manufacturers are working hard to develop new ready-made products for people to buy which use fruits and vegetables in unusual ways.

Your challenge is to make a presentation to a manufacturer with a new salad that you have designed and made, which looks good and appeals to its customers. It will be sold in supermarkets. The manufacturer wants you to use fruit and vegetables from different parts of plants, such as roots, leaves, fruits, . . . The salad should have a low fat salad dressing to go with it.

In shops and restaurants there is a wide range of salads, using different fruits and vegetables

Why this activity is useful

You will find out some important information about eating in a healthy way. You will also find out about the origins of some of the foods we eat, and how this can affect the way we prepare them, and about the **nutritional** changes that can happen when we process food. Finally you will use several ways of finding out (researching) about food and discovering what people need from their food. You will learn how to present food in an exciting and interesting way.

The broader picture . . .

◆ Are there more adverts for fast food and sweets than for salads? Why do you think this is so?

◆ Why do people buy ready-made salad dressings when we can quickly make them ourselves from simple and cheap ingredients?

◆ Fresh strawberries are available all year. Where do they come from when they are not in season here? Is this the same for other fruits?

To be successful

You will need to:

★ use your research and knowledge about healthy eating to help you to design a healthy salad with a dressing. It should look appetizing and make customers want to buy it

★ experiment with combinations of colours, textures, shapes and flavours

★ record what you do, your thoughts, your ideas and your tests. You should then present your record to the manufacturer in a professional way.

Planning things through

Investigating fruits and vegetables and finding out about healthy eating are important to this challenge. Some of these tasks may be carried out in groups. If you do this then you will be able to share information and skills as you design and make a quality product.

▶ Your teacher will help you to make a plan to meet your deadline.

▶ Don't forget you will need to experiment with possible ideas, and do taste tests with your class as well as evaluating your final salad and dressing.

Finding out about fruits and vegetables

Many students find sharing tasks and information a quick way to do research.

It is vital that we understand the materials (that is the food) that we use.

Collect five to six very different fruits and vegetables. Ask your teacher if you need help.

Look at each one carefully and record what you discover on a chart like the one below. The background information may help. Don't forget to label the part of the plant that it comes from.

Name of fruit or vegetable	Horizontal section	Vertical section	Background info.
CUCUMBER FRUIT — remains of flower	skin — seeds	seeds →	stalk ← PEA ← fruit — CAULIFLOWER — leaves — leaves — CARROT ← roots → — ONION

Preparing fruits and vegetables

Take a fruit or vegetable and decide the best way to cut it into even-sized pieces to get a good shape. (Think back to the fruits and vegetables you looked at above, and the notes you made about their structure.) Can you cut it in another way to get a different effect?

The safest way to cut an onion into small pieces is shown in the drawings below. But you can also cut an onion into rings.

Try out your ideas practically. Suggest ways of cutting fruits and vegetables which will make them look unusual and attractive in a salad. Are there any parts which you should not eat? Are there any fruits or vegetables which are not suitable for cutting?

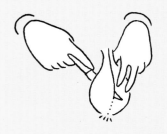

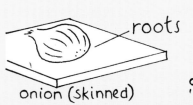

roots

onion (skinned)

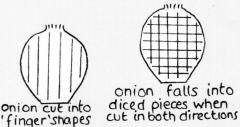

onion cut into 'finger' shapes

onion falls into diced pieces when cut in both directions

The story of Marks and Spencer ribbon vegetables

Joanne Catmull (Corporate Publicity) describes the development of their new product.

Following our success in selling a range of ready-prepared fruits and vegetables we launched **ribbon vegetables**.

We wanted to offer a unique product that would give our customers something that would be difficult and expensive to make at home. We could also offer excellent value as our customers would have no waste or preparation time.

We found a piece of catering equipment used by restaurants to 'ribbon' vegetables and used this to produce a small quantity which we sold in some of our stores as a **trial**. The vegetables were very popular so we challenged our supplier – Tinsley – to develop a piece of equipment that would replicate the action of the catering equipment but on a much larger scale. We needed a ribboning machine that would produce large amounts economically with a minimal need for manual labour.

Our supplier rose to the challenge and they now peel, 'ribbon' and pack just over 1 tonne of vegetables exclusively for Marks and Spencer every day.'

MARKS & SPENCER

How can you make your idea original and different?

Finding out what people like or want

Before you start to design your salad you must have clear ideas about what people want in a salad if it is going to be popular.

Find out what people would like in the new salad you are developing. Ask them to taste some ready-made salads to find out their preferences and opinions.

When you have found this out make a list or **spider diagram** of the key things that people want. Use your list or diagram to help you decide what to put into your salad.

Designing skills:
Researching information
89

What is a salad and what is a salad dressing?

Before you start to design anything it is always a good idea to find out about what already exists. Here are some ways you could do this (but you may have your own ideas).

Finding recipes

Look in **recipe** books and use the index section to find the salads and salad dressings. Find at least five totally different types of salads and five different types of salad dressings. They may use very different foods, or use cooked or uncooked foods, or only one type of food, or be eaten hot or cold . . . Find lots of ideas.

When you've decided which salads best show what a salad can be, record them in an interesting and brief way. Labelled food drawings are very useful.

Looking at ready-made salads

Many people buy ready-made salads from supermarkets. If you are trying to develop a new product you need to investigate (look at) what exists already.

Looking at the packets can be very helpful. There are laws about what has to be written on food packaging. Manufacturers must list the **ingredients** they use. The list must start with the ingredient (the food) they use most of, and the other ingredients must be written in order as well, until the last ingredient listed is the one they use least of. This is called listing in descending order.

To help you come up with your own designs, look at examples of ready-made salads and make a list of the ingredients they contain.

Take to pieces (disassemble) some ready-made salads. Weigh each ingredient, and record your findings in descending order, noting the name of the food and the amount. You may want to work out the percentage and record that as well. When you have finished you should consider and discuss:

- what you have discovered
- what type of foods are in the largest amounts
- why?

Ready-made salads can be bought fresh from the chiller cabinets or in cans

Understanding about healthy eating

Healthy eating is one of the most important ways we can help ourselves to feel and be well. Healthy eating often means just making small changes in the meals we eat – eating a little more of some kinds of foods and a little less of others. *The Health of the Nation* report by the Department of Health gives us advice about eating. Here is a summary of some of the advice. You could find out more as part of your research.

Eight guidelines for a healthy diet

1 Enjoy your food

2 Eat a variety of different foods

3 Eat the right amount to be a healthy weight

4 Eat plenty of foods rich in **starch** and **fibre**

5 Don't eat too much **fat**

6 Don't eat sugary foods too often

7 Look after the **vitamins** and **minerals** in your food

8 If you drink alcohol, keep within sensible limits

Tips about healthy eating

Grill food instead of frying it

Cut fat off meat

Use low fat spreads and milks

Eat fish, poultry, and lean cuts of meat

Go easy on cakes and biscuits, try fruit instead

Try to eat at least four slices of bread each day

Eat plenty of vegetables and salads

(Sources *Food Sense*, Ministry of Agriculture and Fisheries and *Health of the Nation and You*, Department of Health)

How healthy is your salad?

You could find out how healthy your salad and salad dressing is by using a database on a computer, or food tables, to show you how much fat, fibre, Vitamin C and other **nutrients** there are in your chosen design.

Designing a salad dressing

Sometimes salad ingredients taste or work better with a dressing. For example a dressing can:

- help them stick together
- make them taste better
- stop them drying out.

Most salad dressings are mixtures of oils (such as sunflower oil, or olive oil) and waters (such as vinegar, or fruit juice).

What happens when you try to mix oil and water?
Oil and water will separate unless you add an **emulsifier**. This can be an ingredient such as egg yolk or mustard.

Most salad dressings are **emulsions**. You can create your own interesting recipes by mixing different oils with different fruit juices or flavoured vinegars, and adding an emulsifier.

There are many ready-made salad dressings to chose from, but it is easy to make your own, too.

Puzzling boxes

Your challenge!

The idea of gifts and toys packaged inside special containers is not a new idea. Kinder® Eggs, for example, have used this idea by producing a chocolate egg with a toy or puzzle inside. Jack-in-the-boxes and lucky dips also rely on the delight people take in surprises. The excitement of opening a mystery box and finding a surprise inside is something both adults and children enjoy. It's like opening a surprise Christmas present!

This challenge is unlike many in this book as it places many **constraints** on you such as being told the size of box you are going to make. But it also gives you an opportunity to use advanced technology in your making.

There is still a challenge – to design an interesting surprise puzzle that is suitable for computer-aided manufacturing and which fits inside a wooden box. This box can be **detailed** to suit the design of your puzzle.

The other challenge is to work more accurately than you ever have before!

Why this activity is useful

Designers use accurate drawings and 3-D models to develop a design. They help to make sure that the final product will do the job it is intended to do. Your puzzle must be accurate if it is to work properly and it must fit your box. The modelling techniques that you are going to learn in this project will be ones that you will need to use many times in the future.

This challenge also introduces you to **computer-aided design and manufacture**. So when you have done the challenge you will be ready to use computers in D & T again in the future.

CAD being used to design helicopter parts at Westland Aerospace

Hand carved box made to hold a
Beatrix Potter collection set

The broader picture . . .

In the past it was a tradition to make gifts to give to friends and relatives, especially at Christmas.

Nowadays, most of the gifts we give are bought and usually only exclusive, expensive products are hand made.

◆ What sort of image does the term 'hand made' have for you?

◆ Are there any gifts you could make for someone in your life?

◆ Which sort of gift do you think means the most?

To be successful

Accuracy is the most important thing in this project. Your design **portfolio** needs to show how you made sure you were accurate in:

★ your drawings

★ your cutting out of card models

★ getting your box and puzzle to go well together.

You need to ask yourself questions to check how successful your manufactured puzzle is:

★ Do the pieces fit together well?

★ Is the puzzle design interesting/challenging?

★ Is it made as well as you would expect from a shop?

★ Does the finished item look like the design proposals?

Planning things through

There is a lot of work to be done in this challenge and you may need to work on more than one job at a time. You should be able to keep working while you are waiting to use special tools or machinery. Make sure your plans show how you will make this happen.

Generating and developing ideas for your puzzle

Your puzzle will be made from flat pieces of plastic sheet. It might take the form of a jigsaw-type puzzle, or be a series of **geometric** shapes that the user can put together to make a 3-D object. The puzzle should be difficult to complete or should stimulate the imagination of the user you design it for.

Who will use the puzzle and the box? Who might want such an item?

Brainstorming might help you produce a lot of possible answers to these questions quickly. Try this with a few friends, but be sure to keep a note of all the ideas that you have.

> Designing skills:
> Using other people   91

There are some brainstorming rules in the *designing processes* section that will help you. Quick sketches are all you need at the moment. Write notes alongside your ideas to explain the reasons why you think they are good or not so good.

Do not throw away *any* of your first ideas. They are a very important part of the design folio that you should develop in all your challenges.

A sheet full of ideas should only take you about 15 to 20 minutes to produce. Remember it's having *several* ideas that's important at this stage.

3-D modelling ideas for your puzzle

Start modelling your ideas in 3-D as soon as possible. Sketch with scissors and card. Modelling in card also helps develop your ideas further – you can check that they will work BEFORE you start to make them in the final material.

One thing to check by modelling is that your puzzle will fit into the size of box you are making. Start with pieces of card which will fit exactly in the box.

> Designing skills:
> Modelling in card   105

This would be a good time to use templates (either commercial plastic ones or ones made from carefully cut pieces of card) in your designing, if you are drawing (or cutting) repeating shapes.

Designing the puzzle using computer-aided design (CAD)

CAD stands for **computer-aided design**. CAD is being used more and more widely in industry to design products. You will be drawing your puzzle with CAD software and then cutting it out with a machine that uses your computer file.

The advantages of using CAD

CAD has many advantages over designing on paper. Some of these are very similar to the advantages of using a word-processor instead of a typewriter. For example:

● You can draw ideas on screen and change them many times until they are right.

● You can make changes that make sure that you are not wasting the materials.

● You can save your designs on disk, and use and modify them time and time again.

● You can make the designs bigger or smaller, just like the letters in a piece of writing.

CAD in action at Westland Aerospace

Geometric shapes offer a lot of possibilities that you can use as you develop your puzzle. Do you have any templates that you could use to help you produce shapes such as squares, circles, triangles, etc.?

You need to keep the individual shapes simple because they are likely to fit together better and can be used in many different combinations.

As you develop initial ideas keep checking that they are suitable for the intended user.

Using card is a good way of testing on others how hard it is to do the puzzle, before you finalise your design.

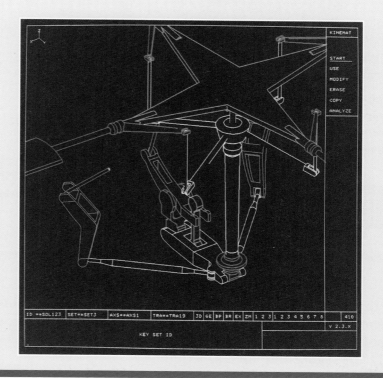

Designing the puzzle using computer-aided design (CAD)

■ You can make families of designs from your original design.

Thinking about production on CAD

You can also use your CAD software to design for manufacture by considering these questions:

Designing skills:
Thinking about production **109** ➤

■ The milling machine can cut out a lot of pieces from one sheet. How can you reduce the time that the milling machine will take to cut them all out?

■ When cutting out a dress from a piece of fabric, a tailor arranges the pattern pieces to make sure there is as little waste as possible. How can you do the same with your arrangement of shapes on the piece of polystyrene sheet?

■ If you make a 3-D construction puzzle in 1 mm polystyrene sheet you will need a 1 mm cutter to produce the slots. Why?

For this task you need to use either a two-dimensional (2-D) drawing package on your school's computers, or the CAD software of a CAD/CAM machine such as a milling machine.

You will transfer the ideas that you developed on paper and then card to the computer screen.

Making the puzzle using computer-aided manufacture (CAM)

CAM stands for **computer-aided manufacture**. In this case the manufacturing machine is a milling machine. A computer controls where the cutter moves to, when to cut, how deep to cut and when not to cut. It will cut out the EXACT shapes that you have designed using CAD.

CAD in the disk case challenge 39

A computer-controlled milling machine allows you to produce a lot of pieces which are identical in shape and size.

There are several different types of milling machines in schools so your teacher will need to show you the milling machine that you are going to work on.

Remember the success of your CAM work depends upon having designed for production at the CAD stage.

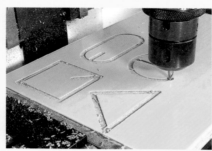
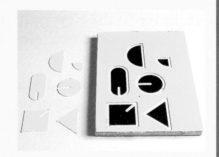

Evaluating yourself

The *To be successful* box on the *Challenge* page gave you a number of questions to ask yourself. Use them in completing your **evaluation** sheet.

Designing skills: Evaluating yourself 122

KEY
1 – Poor
5 – Excellent

NAME	Sanjay	Winston	Julie	Bina
How did the pieces fit together?	3	4	2	5
Is the puzzle a challenge?	2	3	4	4
Does the puzzle look like the design?	4	3	4	4
How well made is the puzzle?	3	4	3	4

All wrapped up

Your challenge!

People eat different types of pasties all over the world, but they are not always called 'pasties'. Jamaican patties, samosas, pancake rolls, and burritos all have an outside case made from flour and water, and a filling inside, just like a 'pasty'.

A food manufacturer makes savoury pasties but the sales team has reported a drop in sales. The manufacturer wants to develop a new pasty to add to its range to attract more customers. It can't change the **production line** in the factory so the new pasty must use the usual bought-in ready made wholemeal pastry. However, it can change the filling.

Your challenge is to design a new and appetising filling for the pasty which customers will want to buy.

You'll develop your ideas by tasting other pasties and finding out what customers want.

You'll experiment with different ingredients for fillings and test them to help you to design something new and tasty for the customers.

You'll need to work out the cost of the filling to make sure that the pasties won't cost too much in the shop, so customers want to buy them, and so the company will make a **profit**.

Why this activity is useful

You will work as part of a **product development team** which will help you to understand how much time and work goes on behind the scenes when developing new food products.

You will get practise in researching and developing ideas and being creative.

You will understand more about how different ingredients behave and how you can develop a product to a **specification**. Professional designers often redevelop part of a product rather than starting from scratch.

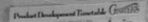

The broader picture . . .

Cornish miners are famous for eating pasties. Their pasties were savoury at one end and sweet at the other end.

◆ Can you find out whether they were the first to eat pasties?

◆ How did this type of pasty meet their needs?

◆ What other foods do you know, or can you find out about, that are like pasties – a meal in a portable container that you can eat?

As well as meat pasties, companies now make vegetable pasties and use wholemeal pastry.
Why do you think this is?

To be successful

Your class or a group will present a design proposal for a new filling.

★ The filling should be developed from your research into what exists already and what customers want and will pay for.

★ It will be appetizing and interesting.

★ You will work out how to produce a number of pasties with identical fillings.

★ You should test your pasty on potential customers, and record their reactions.

Planning things through

You need to check your deadline to plan enough time to:

❱ carry out research and to look at your results

❱ develop a number of ideas for the filling and test them

❱ produce the best pasty.

What can be done for homework to speed things along? Your teacher may share out different tasks amongst your group. What tasks will you undertake?

Bright ideas

Product development begins with generating ideas. You need to have lots of different ideas to achieve one or two excellent ones. Where do new ideas come from?

■ Brainstorming in a group.

■ Finding out what customers think with **surveys** and **questionnaires**, or by looking at customer complaints.

■ Evaluating existing products and suggesting ways of improving them.

Designing skills: Using other people 91

You should try some or all of these techniques to help you to develop new ideas for your pasty filling.

You could share these tasks between the members of your group.

Market Research 1 What already exists? What's it like?

Look at the range of pasties that you can buy. Different shops sell pasties in a variety of fillings and shapes.

Working in teams or a group, collect a range of pasties and analyse them.

You need to look at the pasties closely and set up a **taste panel**.

Produce a chart to show what you found out about each pasty. It should include:

size   weight   cost
appearance   texture
taste   colour

Write a short report or give a presentation about the range of pasties already on the market. What suggestions can you make to extend the range of fillings?

Is there a gap in the market? Can you suggest something that will tempt people to try something new?

Market Research 2   What do customers want?

Tastes vary from person to person. Your job is to find a filling which appeals to a lot of people or to a particular group of people (such as vegetarians or teenagers).

Carry out some research to find out the kinds of fillings **consumers** would like to buy.

Finding out what customers want

Investigating pasty fillings

Find out how pasty fillings are made. Look at a range of recipes or labels on ready-made pasties.

- What foods or ingredients are used?
- How are they prepared?
- What does each ingredient do?
- Why is it included?
- How much does it cost?

Draw up a chart to show your results.

Suggest other ingredients which you could include to make your pasty original.

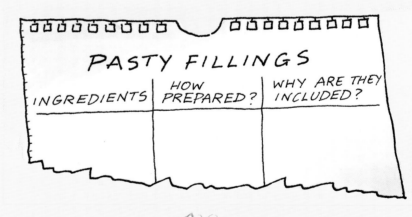

PASTY FILLINGS

INGREDIENTS	HOW PREPARED?	WHY ARE THEY INCLUDED?

Sorting out the good ideas

When you have a number of ideas you must sort out which will be the best ones. This is called **concept screening**. Out of 60 ideas only one or two will get through to sell in a shop. You have to decide which ideas meet the challenge the best. (Re-read the *Challenge* and see which of your ideas meet it.)

Which ideas will appeal to consumers the most?

Which ideas can you make and sell at a price which consumers will like?

Will the ingredients or raw materials be easy to find?

Designing skills:
Evaluating ideas

121

Writing a specification

Once you have found out what exists already and what people want, you can write a specification for a new pasty filling. This shows what the new pasty filling will be like.

- How will it taste?

- What will it look like?

- What will the texture be like?

- How much filling should there be?

- How much should the filling cost?

SPECIFICATION FOR A 'SCHOOL LUNCH BOX MINI – PASTY' FILLING.

TASTE – Meaty or cheesy, strong flavour, some spices or herbs to give flavour. Not too salty.

APPEARANCE – a mixture of colours, not oily.

TEXTURE – not too dry, nor runny, mixture of crunchy vegetables and melted cheese.

FILLING – at least 10g – should not shrink too much when cooked.

COSTS – between 25 – 30p. Less than 3g. fat

Prototyping – trying some ideas

When you've written a specification you'll then be able to develop some fillings which try to meet this specification.

If it's got to be like this, how will I make it?

- How will you make your new filling?

- What ingredients will you choose?

- How much will you have of each ingredient?

- How will you prepare it?

Record the ingredients and stages for each filling you try. Afterwards test each filling to see if it meets your specification.

If your ideas don't work try to think why this is so.

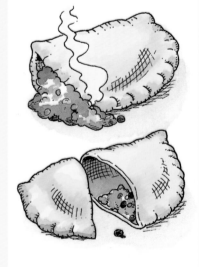

Consumer testing

Do your potential customers like the product? How will you find out?

Taste panel

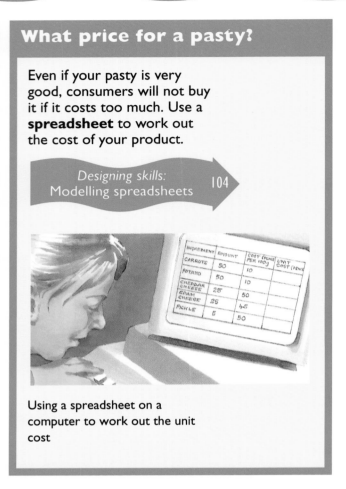

What price for a pasty?

Even if your pasty is very good, consumers will not buy it if it costs too much. Use a **spreadsheet** to work out the cost of your product.

Designing skills: Modelling spreadsheets 104

Using a spreadsheet on a computer to work out the unit cost

Ginsters Ltd

Ginsters are **brand leaders** in the pasty market. Graham Cornish (Product Development Manager) tells us how they developed their new pasty.

The Cheese and onion pasty

Our vegetarian pasties were selling well, but our sales team told us that people had asked for one that was bigger than our 'Ploughman's Pasty', and which really tasted of cheese and onion.

We carried out a lot of research and tested different recipes to get the right filling.

The cheese was important – it had to taste good and to melt when it was cooked, but without being too oily. We use a mixture of three different cheeses and a hint of Dijon mustard.

Once the recipe was right we worked out how we could produce it in large numbers to the same standard. This involved some new production techniques for preparing the cheese and decorating the pastry.

A Ginsters cheese and onion pasty

Quality control

The most difficult part of producing pasties in large quantities is making sure they are all the same. Too little filling and your customers will not be happy, too much filling and the pasties will burst and you will not be able to sell them.

Making a pasty is a step-by-step process. Write your process into a flow chart and try to work out ways to make sure your pasties will all come out the same.

A process flow diagram

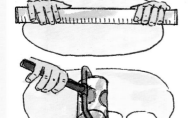

Quality control

Crushing for tomorrow

Your challenge!

Our world cannot go on for ever if we keep on digging up raw materials and using energy in wasteful ways. We owe it to future generations to do something to save the world's natural resources.

On average, 200 billion cans of drink are produced in the world every year.

The recycling of **aluminium** cans has proved to be highly successful. The major aluminium manufacturers tell us that 80 per cent of their product is made from **recycled** material. However, too many people still dispose of aluminium cans with their general household waste, rather than keeping them separate for recycling.

Cans are bulky items to store, and people find it difficult to be sure what material their cans are made of.

A practical way of helping overcome the problem of storage would be to design and make a device that can be used by anybody to crush aluminium cans.

Your challenge is to do just that!

You might also be able to help people know which cans are made of aluminium.

Why this activity is useful

You will use **levers** and **linkages** during this project, which will give you an understanding of how they make things easier to use (they give **mechanical advantage**).
You often need to join together components so that they can still move (this is called making **mechanisms**). This project will help you understand some ways in which this can be done.

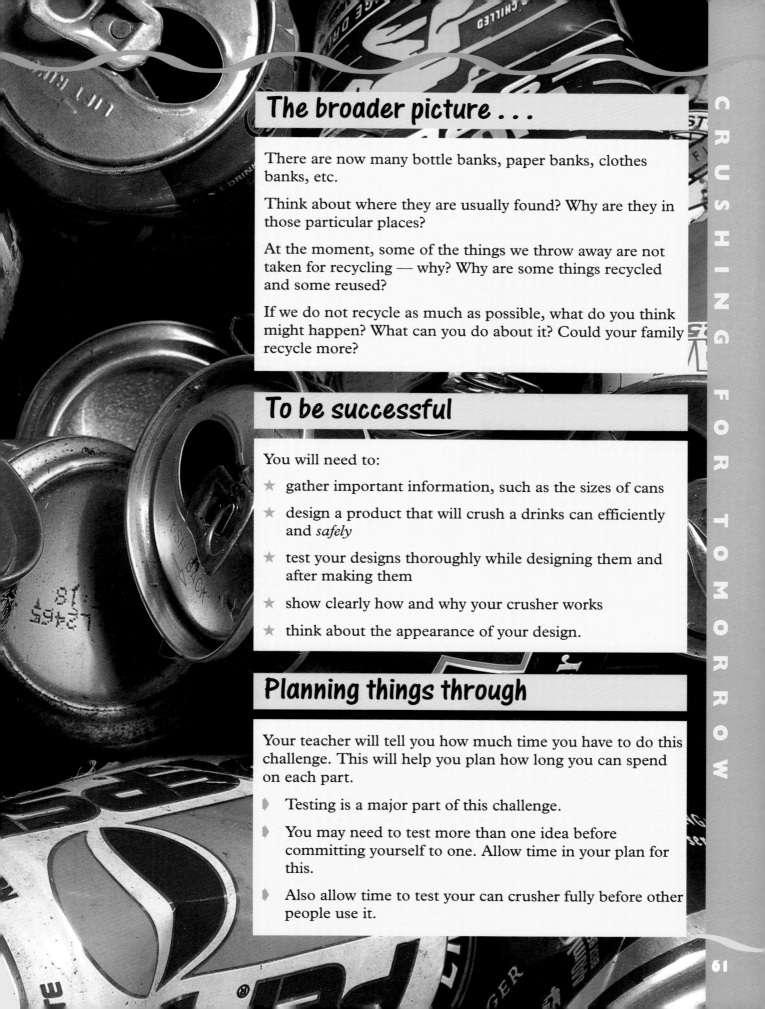

The broader picture . . .

There are now many bottle banks, paper banks, clothes banks, etc.

Think about where they are usually found? Why are they in those particular places?

At the moment, some of the things we throw away are not taken for recycling — why? Why are some things recycled and some reused?

If we do not recycle as much as possible, what do you think might happen? What can you do about it? Could your family recycle more?

To be successful

You will need to:

★ gather important information, such as the sizes of cans

★ design a product that will crush a drinks can efficiently and *safely*

★ test your designs thoroughly while designing them and after making them

★ show clearly how and why your crusher works

★ think about the appearance of your design.

Planning things through

Your teacher will tell you how much time you have to do this challenge. This will help you plan how long you can spend on each part.

▶ Testing is a major part of this challenge.

▶ You may need to test more than one idea before committing yourself to one. Allow time in your plan for this.

▶ Also allow time to test your can crusher fully before other people use it.

The structure of tubes

Cans are **tubes**. Tubes are very strong structures. A flower stalk which stands up to gale force winds is little more than a collection of very thin walled tubes stuck together.

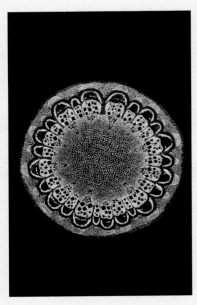

The mass of thin tubes that make up a sunflower stalk

Tubes have the advantage that they are much lighter than a solid **rod** of the same material. But are they stronger or weaker than the rod?

This task allows you to test whether hollow tubes are weaker or stronger than solid rods. The test is simple but fair.

You will be given a rod and a tube made of the same material and with the same **diameter**.

Follow the steps shown and record your results in a table.

How to test the strength of a tube and a rod

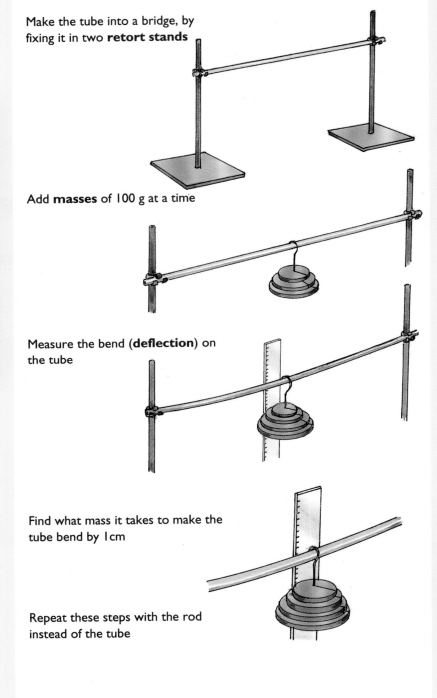

Make the tube into a bridge, by fixing it in two **retort stands**

Add **masses** of 100 g at a time

Measure the bend (**deflection**) on the tube

Find what mass it takes to make the tube bend by 1 cm

Repeat these steps with the rod instead of the tube

What did you discover about the strength of tubes when compared to solid rods?

Investigating the structure of a drinks can

Try using your own strength to crush a can.

■ Put an aluminium drinks can *on its side* and crush it with your hands. Where and how does it resist crushing the most?

■ Stand another drinks can *on its end* with a piece of wood on top. Stand on it to crush it. Feel how it collapses.

How does this compare with doing it by hand?

■ Do the same but with the can on its side.

Now make a drawing of the two crushed cans and answer these simple questions.

■ Which way of crushing left the can taking up least space?

■ In which direction was the can easiest to crush?

■ Which direction produced the safest shape of crushed can?

■ What type of structure is a drinks can — is it a frame or a shell?

■ What other structures are similar to a drinks can but made of different material(s)?

■ What can you say about the strength of the structure of a drinks can?

Electric Buggy challenge 66

Investigating levers

The simplest example of a lever is a children's seesaw. This is usually a straight plank which has a point in the middle where it **pivots**. When you push down on one end, the other end goes up.

The human skeleton is a mass of levers, which allow us to move and do different things. One part of the skeleton that acts as a pivot point is your elbow. Imagine you are lifting a dumb-bell in the fitness room at a local sports centre like the person in the picture. If you could see under your skin this is what you would see.

In this example the biceps muscle is making an **effort** to lift the **load** of the dumb-bell.

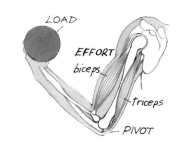

The elbow itself is the **pivot** point. If you look at any lever in operation you will always find a pivot, the load and some effort.

There are three types of lever. In the example the, effort is applied between the pivot and the load. This is known as a **third class lever**.

The following diagrams show other types of lever where the order is different.

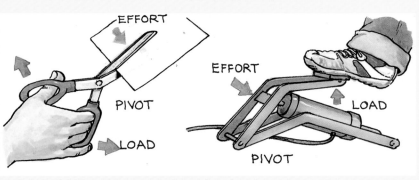

Using your knowledge of levers to design a crusher

You now know more about levers and the way that they can do some work for us.

In designing your crusher you should be able to answer these questions:

◼ What sort of lever are you using in your crusher?

◼ What kind of structure will hold the can while you crush it?

◼ What **linkages** will make your crusher easier to use?

◼ What have you done to make the design safe to use?

◼ What tests have you done to prove your design?

You should answer all these questions on a detailed drawing of your final design.

Making a can crusher

Before talking to your teacher about how you are going to go about making your design, think about these things:

◼ What materials do you need? Make a list.

◼ What materials are available? Check.

List the steps you'll follow as you design and make your crusher, in the order you'll be doing them. You can do this as homework.

Here are some likely ones:

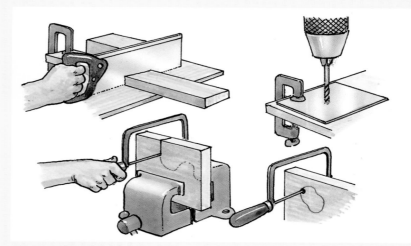

Cutting, shaping and drilling materials

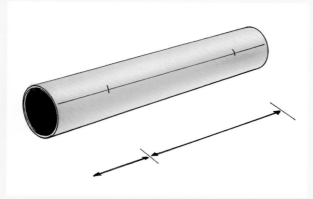

Marking out where to drill a tube

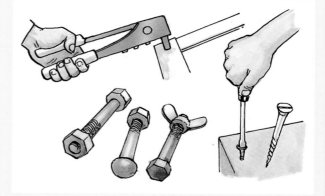

Select the fixings you'll use, such as rivets, nuts and bolts

Evaluation – comparative testing

The simplest way to test your class's designs is to use each of them and see which one works the best – this is called **comparative testing**.

Some of you could do a comparative test and record the results in a chart that shows how you evaluated various features.

COMPARATIVE TEST	SANJAY	WINSTON	JULIE	BINA
HOW WELL IT CRUSHED THE CAN	3			
STRENGTH NEEDED	4			
SAFETY	2			
HOW WELL MADE?	4			
SIZE				
APPEARANCE				

KEY 1-POOR 5-EXCELLENT

This evaluation tests all aspects of the crushers at once. However, one crusher may have the best design but might fail because it is not well made. Here is a more scientific way to look at just one aspect of the crushers.

Measuring forces

The **force** that your crusher puts onto the can is much greater than the force you apply with your arm. This is because the crusher works as a **force multiplier**. The greater the multiplication, the easier it will be to use the crusher.

One way to **evaluate** the crusher is to measure the force that your can crusher is producing and how easy it is to produce that force (its **mechanical advantage**).

You need to measure how much effort you have to put into your crusher to make it work (the effort force). Then measure how much force the crusher puts onto the can (the load force).

How much bigger is the load force than the effort force?

Find the most efficient crusher in the class. The diagram below shows how you could set up a test rig to do this.

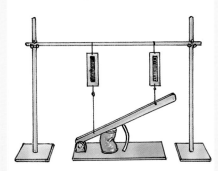

$$\text{Mechanical advantage} = \frac{\text{crushing force}}{\text{hand force}}$$

You should measure everybody's crushers and work out whose crusher is the best **force multiplier**. You could record your results in a chart:

COMPARING MECHANICAL ADVANTAGE			
DESIGNER	CRUSHING FORCE ÷	HAND FORCE =	MECHANICAL ADVANTAGE
SANJAY			
WINSTON			
JULIE			
BINA			

Be careful! The best force multiplier is not necessarily the best can crusher. This is only one way to test your crushers. There are some other questions in this book to help you to evaluate your product.

Designing skills:
Evaluating your product 122

Extending your evaluation

What other questions can you ask about your crushers? Safety will be important.

You are not likely to find the one best product from the class, as some of you may have designed to different **priorities**. For example, a kitchen crusher should look better than one designed for a garage, but the garage one might be more powerful.

What did you set out to achieve? Have you done this?

You could extend your evaluation by seeing which crusher is working best after a month of use. This would evaluate its **durability**.

Finally, you could write a review of your design – summarise its best and worst features.

Super structures

Your challenge!

There are many different types of road vehicles but there are just two main ways in which they are built, both of which focus on making them strong and rigid. One type is built on a framework called a **chassis**. The second type uses the body like a shell, to hold it together and make it stiff.

The world's oil reserves are being used up and designers are giving more attention to developing electrically-powered cars. The latest electric cars can travel at 120 kph and have a range of hundreds of miles between battery charges.

Your challenge is to design and construct an electrically-powered buggy with a hand controller. It should have a body supported on a chassis structure. If you are skilful and have the time you will be able to add other electrical devices to your buggy and make it more personal.

Why this activity is useful

This challenge will require you to work on two very important types of structure. The chassis of your space buggy is a **frame structure**. You will also learn about **shell structures**.

You will be doing some useful work on electrical control.

You'll use the knowledge gained in these two areas again and again in Design and Technology.

The winner is the car that can travel furthest on a pint of petrol

The broader picture . . .

More and more people have their own cars. Many families now have two cars. Can we really go on producing enough cars for everyone to have their own?

Some people say that electrically-powered vehicles are more environmentally friendly. Do you think that this is true?

Formula One racing cars have some of the strongest shell structures built. Some people think that motor racing is a waste of the earth's valuable resources, whilst others say that it helps us find new answers to technological problems. What do you think?

To be successful

You'll have made a buggy which not only works well, but also looks good. Your buggy should be able to pass some of the following tests:

★ be able to go forwards and backwards

★ have sound or lights

★ have an attractive or special shape that you can explain.

By the end of the project you should also be able to:

★ explain the difference between frame and shell structures and recognise them in other natural or man-made things

★ use a circuit diagram to explain to others how your vehicle is controlled.

Planning things through

▶ For this challenge you may use new skills. Start your planning by trying to decide what they may be and when you will need to learn them.

▶ Make a list of the stages of this challenge and how long you will spend on each stage.

▶ Use the *Planning* section of this book to record and evaluate your planning at different stages of the project.

Identifying structures

Your buggy's chassis is going to be a frame structure.

Frame structures

Frame structures can be man-made or natural. They are made up of separate parts called **members**. If you look at a frame structure it is easy to see these separate members. But frames are often hidden because they hold up surfaces (such as a building or car body) and because they do not look very attractive.

Shell structures

Shell structures can also be man-made or natural. They are not usually made up of separate parts but are strong shapes in themselves. The surface holds itself up by the way it is shaped. The word 'shell' will give you a clue to one such natural shape.

> Can crusher challenge 60

An interesting fact

There are more animals in the world with a body shell than any other form of protection. Seven out of ten animals are insects and every one has its own body shell. Shell structures are a natural success story!

A simple test can demonstrate the key to strength in shells.

An empty animal shell

Hold a piece of thin paper by its corner and it will droop down. Hold it so that it curves in the right direction and it will hold its own weight. Curves are the key to strength in shells.

A partly-clad steel roof structure

A quadruped skeleton

An empty car body shell

Testing frame structures

If you make up a simple **rectangular** frame using a construction kit (such as Meccano) or paper fasteners and strips of card, it will distort into a **parallelogram** very easily. Adding one **diagonal** piece or member will stop this. Triangles are the key to strength in frame structures.

Sometimes the triangles used are very small plates which are called **gussets**.

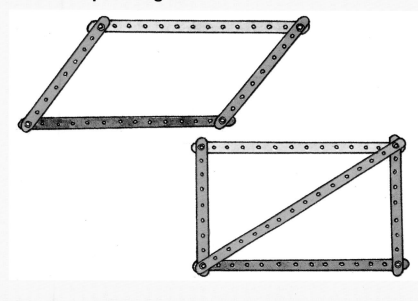

A structure with gusset plates

Your chassis structure must be made to support the rest of the buggy (the load). Loads can be the structure's own weight or a separate weight such as a person sitting on a chair. A chair is a structure which supports a load, and which may have a shell or frame structure. Read this short case study and find the triangles which give the chair strength.

A child's chair

The photo shows a rare child's chair around 200 years old. It is made from elm wood. Its three legs stand perfectly on an uneven floor where a four legged version would wobble.

The chair is able to cope with stresses in all directions because of the thickness of the wood and the way that the different pieces are jointed.

The back of the chair slopes slightly to make it more comfortable, whilst keeping the load that it has to support firmly in the middle of the three sturdy legs.

This piece of furniture was designed to be functional not fashionable. But because its design made it fit for its job, it has now become a valuable antique.

When your buggy is stationary (standing still) and is only carrying its own weight, an engineer would describe it as a **static load**. When you make your buggy run along the ground it becomes a moving load. This is described as a **dynamic load**.

A lot of structures need to support both static and dynamic loads. To carry a dynamic load needs extra strength.

Your buggy needs to be strong enough to cope with both static and dynamic loads.

Designing the buggy chassis

Your chassis will need to fit the following descriptions:

■ It must be strong enough to prevent it being knocked out of shape if it hits an object (remember your knowledge of triangulation).

■ It must be as light as possible.

■ It must support the electric motor firmly.

■ It must allow the electric motor to be connected securely to the back axle by an elastic band.

■ The band should be tight enough to turn the back axle without slipping, so the distance between the motor and the axle is very important.

Using this information, draw up plans for your chassis. Present your plans as an **orthographic drawing** with any notes that you will need.

> Designing skills:
> Drawing systems   98

Controlling your buggy

You can drive your buggy with a very simple electrical circuit that has a battery, a switch and a motor, but this will only allow you to drive your buggy forwards. If you do not know how you would connect a switch, battery and motor read the tasks in the door buzzer challenge.

> Door buzzer challenge   24

If you want to be able to drive your buggy backwards and forwards you need to use two switches: a simple on/off switch and a **changeover switch**.

Two circuit diagrams that show how a changeover switch works

A changeover switch

These diagrams show a changeover switch controlling two light bulbs.

Answer these questions to check if you understand what is happening in this circuit.

■ Can you turn both lights off at the same time?

■ Can you have both lights on at the same time?

■ What is the switch doing to the flow of electric current in this circuit?

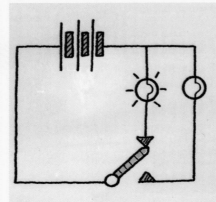
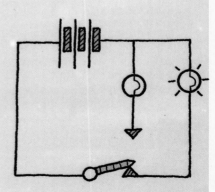

Modelling your buggy circuit

Making your buggy stop and start, as well as go forwards and backwards, involves using two switches in your buggy circuit:

■ the on/off switch to stop and start the buggy

■ a changeover switch to make it go forwards and backwards.

This diagram shows you where to connect your switches to make this circuit.

Connect this circuit together by breadboarding it or by using an electronics kit such as an **Omega board** or an **Alpha board**.

Answer these questions to check if you understand what is happening in this circuit.

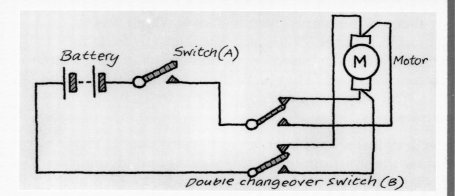

■ Can the motor be made to go forwards and backwards at the same time?

■ Which switch is controlling the direction that the motor spins in?

■ If you wanted to add a buzzer to warn that the buggy was reversing where would you need to connect it?

■ If you wanted to add two white LEDs to the 'forward' circuit to mimic headlights, where would they need to be connected?

Check your answers to these questions at this modelling stage. It will save you a lot of time later.

Personalising your buggy

Adding a body to your buggy

You may have time to add a body to your buggy. If so there are lots of ways you can personalise it.

You could add a body by building curved or flat sheet material (such as card or plastic sheets) onto it piece by piece. This is how cars used to be made.

A better way would be to create a shell by vacuum forming. Remember the buggy will still not be a shell structure because its strength comes from its chassis (its frame).

You can stick card or plastic counters to the body forming with double sided tape to make windows and other features. You can attach plastic counters to your formers to give circular details. What else could you use?

Designing skills:
Using a vacuum former for modelling prototypes 108

Other ideas for making your buggy more personal

Use self-adhesive vinyl to add colour. Cut it using scissors, or you could use a plotter or

cutter controlled by a computer. By using CAD/CAM) you could design and make a drawing template to enable you to produce additional buggy designs or pictures.

Puzzling boxes challenge 46

■ add a warning buzzer that shows the buggy is reversing.

■ add white LEDs to the front and red LEDs to the rear

Classy casting

Your challenge!

Art Deco is the name given to a style which was in fashion during the 1920s and 30s. Designs from this period are usually based on combinations of very simple geometric shapes. They were quite revolutionary at the time. You may recognise some of the items in the pictures.

Jewellery has always been an important part of fashion, adding the finishing touch to an outfit and giving it a special personality. Many designers who worked in the Art Deco style were interested in jewellery and many exciting examples still exist.

Using the pictures of Art Deco designs you will create an attractive item of jewellery which is up-to-date enough to be worn on a special occasion.

Your challenge is to produce a range of design ideas for your jewellery and then produce at least one piece which is beautiful, and beautifully finished.

A magazine cover photo from 1930 showing a model wearing the latest fashion jewellery.

Why this activity is useful

It is very difficult to invent totally original ideas. You will learn how designers use existing ideas to help them to come up with something new. This project will give you experience of reworking old ideas in much the same way as the fashion clothing industry does.

You will learn something about an important period of 20th century design history.

You will also have a special chance to create a very adult design.

You will be introduced to metal **casting**, which is used a lot in industry for making complicated objects.

The broader picture . . .

◆ What do we mean by fashion? You could collect pictures of current fashionable items and make a display that sums up how people your age feel today.

◆ What does Art Deco mean? Was this name given to it to make it sound important?

◆ What was the world like in the 1920s when Art Deco was popular? What major events in history were shortly to follow?

◆ What is it that makes fashion wasteful? Think of the items that you still have at home that you wouldn't wish to admit to your friends.

To be successful

★ Create lots of interesting ideas. Not just one or two!

★ Be sure your own ideas are developed from the historic starting points.

★ Get a really good finish on your casting before you fix it to the **findings**.

★ Produce some jewellery that is very attractive for someone to wear.

Planning things through

Art Deco design ideas are the starting point for your designs.

▶ Where will you get pictures of the Art Deco period from?

▶ When will you do this?

▶ You need to plan time to do this.

▶ Think ahead. How will you present your work for display?

You can save time by doing some of these stages at home.

Visual sources sheet

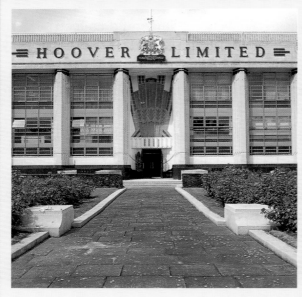

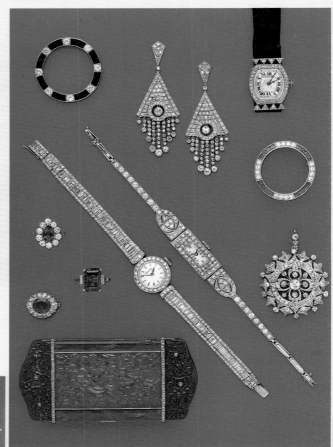

Visual sources for your design from original Art Deco items

Find out what makes Art Deco special and distinctive. Collect some interesting pictures of designs that you like. These examples must be clear; they will contain lots of geometric patterns. Develop your jewellery ideas using these shapes.

Examples of Art Deco jewellery showing geometric patterns

Developing an idea from a picture

Method 1   Simplifying

■ Select the main lines in the picture – these are what you'll base your designs on.

■ It must be possible to make the jewellery all in one piece.

■ You can add to your shape to make it more interesting.

■ Use shapes only – do not add any decoration to the surface as it is very difficult to cut this into the cuttlefish bone which you'll be using as a mould.

■ A simple design gives the best results.

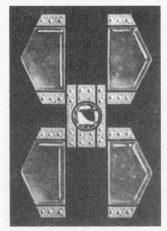

How would you simplify these pieces of jewellery for casting?

Developing an idea from a picture (continued)

Method 2   Masking

1 Choose your source picture.
2 Produce a line diagram to preserve the original (trace it).
3 Use a **mask** so that most of your diagram is hidden and all you can see is an interesting part.
4 Enlarge and adapt that part so that it can become the design for a piece of jewellery in its own right. Remember that you are only going to make one piece so the design must be interesting.

◼ Will you be able to attach your design to the findings?

◼ Try cutting some of your pictures out and mounting them on findings

Jewellery findings enable you to wear your designs without having to make complicated components

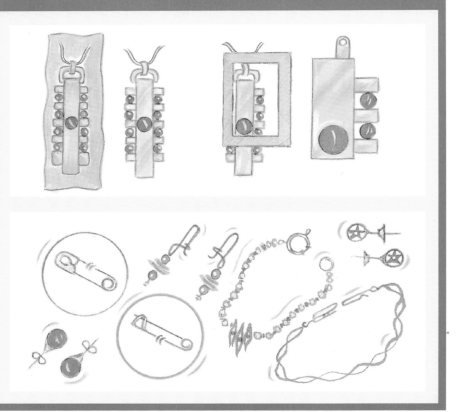

Casting your jewellery

Casting is the traditional method of making complex metal items. It is done by pouring molten metal into a cavity. It is a bit like making jellies or chocolates.

Some metals melt at a lower temperature than others. You may be able to melt aluminium or brass at school in a specially equipped hot working area.

For the jewellery project we are going to use **pewter**, which melts at a comparatively low temperature. You will make the mould from cuttlefish bones like the ones which budgies sharpen their beaks on! The guide on the opposite page shows you how to cast your design.

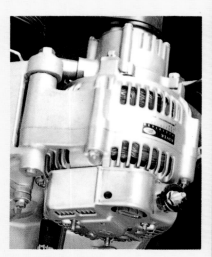

A finished casting

Casting pewter in cuttlefish bone

Product designed and ready for manufacture

Preparing the hardboard backing piece

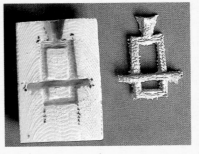

The casting can be released when the metal has cooled and solidified

Flatten one side of the cuttlefish bone on an emery pad

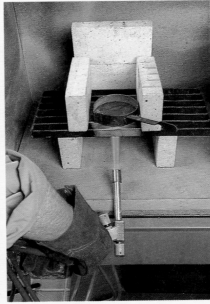
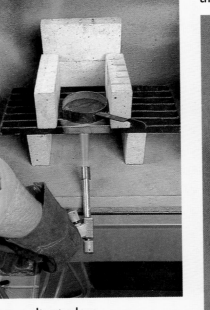

Pewter melts at a low temperature and can be heated on the simplest heat source

You can sculpt the mould with any metal object

A v-shaped gate allows the pewter to flow into the cavity

The pewter is poured in at the gate and allowed to cool

WARNING: Molten pewter causes severe burns! Always wear protective clothing and eye protection when working with any heat source.

Festive food

Your challenge!

Have you got a party or event coming up? Wouldn't it be easy if you could go to a shop and get a box with a selection of food to eat and possibly even serviettes and games? Or would it be better to design and make your own?

Your challenge is to design a range of kits and to develop one example. This should reach a standard suitable for putting on sale in shops. It must have an appropriate selection of food and other contents. The packaging must be effective.

Why this activity is useful

The food and packaging industries often work very closely together. In this project you will learn a lot about the ways that food can be packed to help it stay fresh and to make it look more appealing.

Designers often work as part of a design team – this project will give you experience of this, which you'll use many times in future challenges.

Visual communication is a very important tool for designers. In this project you'll find out about its importance in promoting products.

The broader picture . . .

A good event involves a lot of preparation – kits may help good organisation and be fun. What do you think are their disadvantages?

What big events take place that you think are wasteful? Should they be made illegal?

Do some people do too much at children's parties now with bouncy castles, clowns and expensive presents? Do people enjoy parties where they play pass the parcel, blind man's buff and musical chairs just as much?

Look in your dustbin – a lot of what you have thrown away will be packaging. Should we do more to make sure that packaging can be recycled or reused?

To be successful

★ You will have to work as part of a team to get all the tasks on this challenge done.

★ The package for your kit needs to separate and protect the contents, and attract people to buy it.

★ Everything should look as if it's part of one kit.

★ The food should be attractive and appealing to the people at the occasion it is designed for.

Planning things through

You may have worked as a group with the help of your teacher on other challenges. In this challenge you are going to be working as a team and taking more responsibility for the planning.

Your team will need to plan together:

◗ the content of your kits

◗ what needs to be done

◗ when it has to be done by

◗ how you are going to divide up the work between you

◗ who is going to do each bit.

What sort of event? What sort of people?

Your first action must be to select the event that you will prepare your kits for.

A spider diagram would help.

Think of a number of events that would benefit from a kit. Put each one in the centre of a spider. On each leg add:

■ Who goes to these events?

■ How would they be dressed?

■ Where they would eat – standing? sitting? what on?

■ Is it a happy occasion, or sad?

■ What sort of food would be suitable?

■ What else would be needed for this kit?

■ What sort of image might be suitable?

■ What sort of colours might be suitable?

■ How would the party-goers transport the kit – by car? train? rucksack? pocket?

Designing skills: Researching information 89

Fine Colour Packaging

Fine Colour Packaging in Nottingham produces packaging solutions for a range of clients companies that make anything from toothbrushes to pork pies. Jed Gisborne (chairman) explains.

"It is essential that as part of the brief we receive the product the company is wanting to sell. To help us design a successful package we must know its shape and weight as well as its size."

The design of the package is a vital part of making someone want to buy it. The photograph shows a solution developed for Marks and Spencer to package a bottle of bucks fizz and a Christmas pudding. Can you say what it is that makes you think this is an authentic Marks and Spencer package? Once all the design aspects of the package are correct the package can go into production. There are four main stages in this process: Printing; Cutting and Creasing; Windowing (this is an optional process); Gluing.

At the end of all this Fine Colour Packaging despatches the flat

packages to its customer, confident that they will receive a high quality and economic solution to their requirements.

Packaging your event kit

Your design will probably have a main package and one or more inner containers for the food and other items. Why do you think this should be so? You could try to make it all in one.

Investigating card outer packages

■ Look at as many different packages as possible.

■ Separate them into food packaging and other packaging.

■ Carefully take the packages apart to see how they are assembled. Do not cut anything when you do this.

■ Make some sketch diagrams of the shapes you get. (In maths this shape would be called a **net**. The packaging industry call it a **carton blank**.)

Do you notice anything different about the food packaging?

What shapes might be useful to you for the articles you will be storing?

Remember:

You are designing a package that will hold different things, one of which is food. What special requirements does food have?

Investigating inner packaging

The job for inner packaging is to separate and protect the different items. The food items should not come into contact with each other – some might be moist or have a smell that will affect other items. The food could also pick up infectious bacteria if it came into contact with items that have been handled.

There is some research that you could do:

■ Look at some food packages to see how they work.

■ Look at plastic trays that contain food – how do they work?

■ Look at boxes for fragile items like glasses – how are they made? How do they keep the glasses apart?

■ Visit a fast-food shop and see how it separates the different items that it sells.

Here are a few questions that you ought to consider in your research:

■ What items of food are you going to put into your kit?

■ How much of each type of food are you going to include?

■ What shapes and volumes will the food items take up?

■ How will you take the food items out of their compartments?

■ What other items are you going to put in your kit?

■ What materials could you use for the different parts of the packaging?

■ How will you keep the items separate?

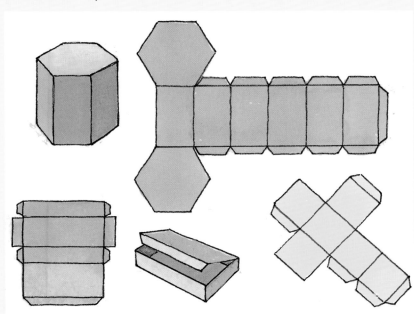

EVENT KITS

Wrappings?

You should consider whether you need to separate any of the contents of your kit by sealed wrappings. Fragile items need protection.

Unlike other things in your event kit, food goes off. It also can spoil other things with its smell, or if it gets mixed up with them. To solve this problem you may need to wrap the food items to completely separate them from each other, and from the other things in your box.

Some ways that food can go off

Some foods lose water and wilt

Some foods attract water and become soggy

Some foods emit strong smells or flavours

Some fatty foods develop a bad taste if stored in light, warm and open places

Yeasts, moulds and bacteria can spoil foods and cause food poisoning in warm damp conditions

Plant and animal cells contain **enzymes** which make some foods go brown when cut or bruised

Now look at the foods that you have chosen to add to your kit. Do you need to take special precautions with any of them?

Deciding on your wrapping choices

■ In one column, make a list of all the wrapping materials that will be available for you to use.

■ In another column next to the first, list the foods you have chosen for your kit.

■ Draw a line from each food item to the wrapping materials that would be suitable for it.

■ Design a fair test to decide which wrapping is best to use for each of your event pack foods

■ Record how you did your tests and your results.

■ List the packagings you might use, then interview your customers to check which will appeal most.

82

Presenting for maximum impact!

The first thing a consumer sees when he or she picks up a product is the way that it is packaged. If it looks good there is a much better chance that the consumer will buy the product. In other words, attractive packaging often means the difference between success and failure when it comes to sales.

Good **graphic design** has several elements which all play a part in the impact a product makes on its possible customers.

Using imagery

To decide what images you want your package to carry you will first need to identify who the package is being aimed at. Here are some general rules that you should try to stick to, with examples of good and not so good approaches to design.

■ The **type** and **lettering** should match the overall style of the packaging.

ARCADIA

Avant Garde

Bodoni

Shelly Volante

■ Try to use no more than two **typefaces**. Avoid similar types such as two **serif fonts** – try to match a serif with a **sans serif** font.

This heading is in Helvetica
This text is in Avant Garde. Both these typefaces are sans serif. Because they look similar to each other, they clash.

These are both sans serif fonts

This heading is in Helvetica
This text is in Times. Times is a serif typeface, Helvetica is a sans serif typeface. Because they look quite different from each other, they complement each other.

Times is a serif font

■ Don't use a traditional, restrained or classical style for your event kit unless this suits the people it is for. Should it be in a modern or fun style?

■ Colour and tone are important. Novel and fun designs should use bright colours or pastel shades of primary colours. It's probably not a good idea to use earthy browns or dull greens unless you want a rural image.

■ Great designs are often borrowed or adapted from the work of others.

Designing skills: Classy casting challenge 72

Use the Art and Design section in your school or local library to look at the work of great artists or designers. Three names that you may not have heard of but might look for are:

Herb Lubalin
Among many other things, Lubalin was a typographer who created many new designs. His best known one is called Avant Garde Gothic which was originally the title of a magazine.

A.M. Cassandre
Cassandre designed many superb posters in the first half of this century. His designs were dynamic and are sought after now as great examples of poster art.

George Lois
An American who produced bold, original and sometimes outrageous designs in the 50s and 60s. Lois is one of the first people to be mentioned as being an inspiration by contemporary graphic designers.

Project evaluation

In this project you did a lot of evaluating as you went along, but when your team have completed the challenge you should all evaluate how successful you were. Also consider what you might do better next time. You should draw up your own list of the aspects of your designing and making that need to be evaluated, but here are a few ideas to start you off.

◼ How well did the food fit in the storage unit?

◼ How good was the appearance or image of the package?

◼ Would it appeal to the intended users?

◼ Was the food tasty and enjoyable?

◼ Were the other items the best ones to include?

Look again at the *To be successful* box next to the *Challenge*.

A very good way to present your evaluation would be by making a group presentation to the rest of the class. This will need teamwork just like the Challenge did!

Designing skills

This second part of the book will help you develop the designing skills you need to carry out the designing and making assignments in the first part. It looks closely at various aspects of designing, which are developed further in the other *Challenges* books.

You may use some of these pages with your teacher when learning more about designing.

Remember – you should *always* turn to this section *before asking your teacher for help* when you are designing and are not sure what to do next.

One of the most important things you should be learning in Design and Technology is to work independently – having your **own** ideas, developing them in your **own** way, understanding for yourself **what** you are doing, and **why** you are doing it that particular way.

This part of the book is divided into sections. Developing ideas is the biggest of these as this is what you should be concentrating on at this stage.

Contents

Clarifying the task

When you start a designing and making task it is easy to be misled. You need to be sure you know what you are really being asked to do in a design brief.

You then need to research information that helps you produce ideas that are appropriate, and well informed.

Knowing what you really need to do

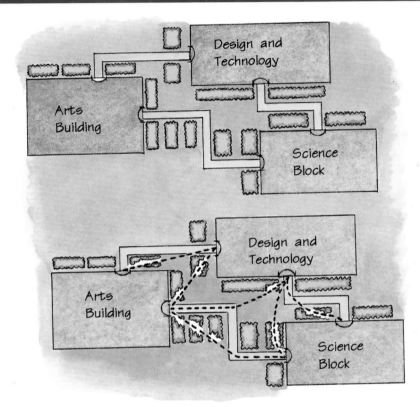

Here's a bird's eye view of a new school, showing the paths between the blocks, and around the flowerbeds

Here are the routes which the new students took. The architect did not bother to find out where the students needed to go. As a result, they were constantly being told to keep off the flowerbeds

Lots of people rush in thinking they know what to do. Often they do not understand the problem well enough to find the best answer. Design and technology is about finding the best answer. To do this you have to know really well what the problem is – this is how you'll get the results you want.

The following list of questions should help you get better results.

1 What exactly do I want to achieve? and perhaps, what am I expected to achieve? (Check the section on *Working with design briefs*.)

2 Is that really what I need to achieve? (Ask yourself again.)

3 What different ways are there to achieve this?

4 Which of these ways is the best?

Now you might be ready to go ahead. The first stage will be to ask yourself,

5 How am I going to do this? (Go back to question 3 again.)

As you work, keep asking yourself,

6 Am I on track to achieve what I need to?

7 If not, how should I change what I am doing?

Afterwards, look back and ask yourself

8 Have I done what I set out to achieve? Be very honest – you probably haven't achieved everything!

CLARIFYING THE TASK

86

People in industry ask questions like these to get things done well. They are based on GRASP (Getting Results and Solving Problems), which was developed by Demetrius Comino, the inventor of Dexion. Here are some things we all do when designing and making. Match them to the eight questions above.

A identify needs
B clarify the task
C generate ideas
D bring ideas together and develop them
E plan how to proceed
F make the developed design
G check progress against the design
H evaluate the product

Comino ran a factory where they were always needing to change things. The products they stored changed all the time, so they often had to change their shelving too.

Once Comino stopped to ask 'What exactly do I want to achieve?' He then saw what the best answer would be – a system of shelving that could be changed around without throwing any of it away. So he invented Dexion (the Greek word for 'right').

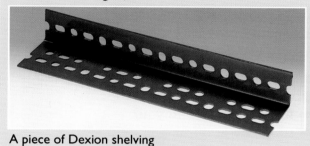

A piece of Dexion shelving

Working with design briefs

In this book there are challenges for you to try. Some of these give you more freedom than others. Your teacher may give you limits to work to – what materials you can use, how big it can be, etc. Sometimes you will be given a **brief** (instructions) to tell you what you are to do.

When you are designing for yourself it is easier to know the best answer to a design problem. But often you will be designing for other people. To do this well you have to find out more about the people you are designing for, and just what their needs are.

Professional designers often work to a brief written by a customer (client) or other people in their own company. Usually they ask the client questions to make the brief clearer. This helps them to understand what they need to do.

Talking to the client may help the client to understand their needs better and they might change the brief.

You could use the questions on the previous page to check what your brief asks of you.

Here is a design brief given by the ceramics manufacturer Thomas to its designers, Queensbury Hunt. Below it are the products that came from it

We require a modern elegant and tranquil shape which is convincing by its sheer clarity and softness of line. Moreover it must be possible to create a variety of decorations for this range as the success of the shape is much contingent on its decoratability

Your teacher may give you a brief. Or you can pretend to be the client and write a brief for yourself. This can help you to be clear about what you are trying to achieve.

How to respond to a design brief

Below are four ways to help you understand a design brief better and to get started on your design ideas.

I Group discussion

You could start with a group discussion, maybe you could discuss the brief with

◆ your teacher and the rest of the class?
◆ a small group of other students?
◆ the person next to you?
◆ someone at home?

Just putting the brief into different words can be useful.

Here is a brief:

> Your brief is to design and make a small chocolate novelty in appropriate packaging that guests can take away from the official opening of a new school.
>
> There are some limits placed on you. The design should be based on the school's crest. 500 will be needed so they must be very inexpensive.

Here are some questions to ask:

◆ Does the brief make sense? (If not ask someone else to help you make sense of it.) – What is a chocolate novelty?
◆ What am I expected to do? – *Design a novelty and its pack for a school, and make them.*
◆ What am I not to do? (Does it place limits on you?) – *Design something expensive.*
◆ What will it look like when I have done it? – *Small, something to do with the school crest.*

◆ What would it look like if I did it really well? – *Very attractive to look at; it would make you want to eat it.*
◆ Am I sure that is what is expected? – *Yes, but I must remember the packaging.*
◆ In what other ways might I approach it? – *I could use the crest on the package only.*
◆ Is there a way of responding to this brief that would really surprise people? – *I could put a small chocolate in a big pack.*
◆ How would I change this brief? – *I think the crest is boring. I am going to check to see if I can base my design on the front view of the school.*

2 Identify the key words:

Pick out the *key words* in a brief (with a highlighter pen, or underline them).

What do they mean? Suggest alternative words. This will draw out the important things to think about:

Your brief is to design and make a small

chocky bar

chocolate novelty in appropriate packaging

that guests can take away from the

opening of a new school.

The design should be based on the school's

badge

crest. 500 will be needed so they must be

cheap

very inexpensive.

3 Look more closely at the situation

Ask yourself about the situation (or context) the design brief comes from.

◆ Describe the situation.
◆ How can you find out more? Who can tell you more about it?
◆ What are the main needs? Who has these needs?
◆ Is there anything special about those people?
◆ What else affects what you might design?
◆ Has anyone else designed something to solve this situation? What? How good was it?
◆ Is there anything else in the context that could give you special help?

4 Use role play

◆ In a role play one person pretends to be the person with the need (e.g. the school Head wants something to give away to everyone at the opening)
◆ the other asks questions to find out what the person's needs are
◆ then, together, you write a brief for a designer to solve the needs.

Looking closely at a brief and asking questions about it is one way of collecting the information you need, if your design is to be the best possible. There are other ways.

Researching information

Before you begin to design, you need to find out as much useful information as you can.

First you need to decide – What do I need to know?

Make a note of your topic in the middle of a **spider diagram**.

Around the web write places or people where you might find useful information:

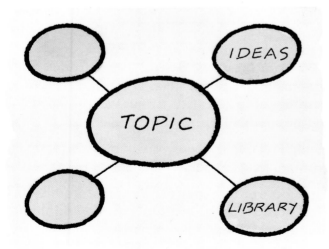

How can you gather and record useful information?
Write a quick list of possibilities.

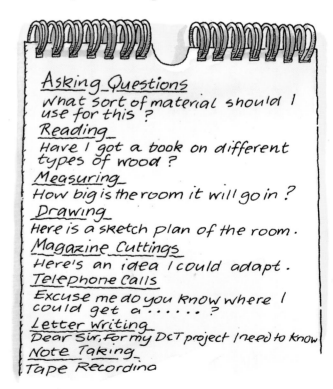

Planning your investigation

Now plan your investigation.

Don't take too much time on this – do as much as you can for homework.

Look at the research grid below to think about the methods you will use. Draw a grid like this and make quick notes of what you do in your information search in the appropriate boxes.

Also keep a time log: note under the clock how long you spent on each activity.

This will help you to learn how long you take researching your design.

Time		Television	Newspapers	Library	Shops	People
	Asking Questions					
	Reading					
	Measuring					
	Drawing					
	Magazine Cuttings					
	Telephone Calls					
	Letters					
	Note Taking					
	Tape recordings					

What products already exist?

Look at existing products (which are similar to yours). These might help you with your designing.

Do they work? Are they good/effective designs? What is wrong with them? How do they work?

Designing skills: Looking at existing products 94

Collect all your information while you are starting to generate design ideas.

Ask yourself: 'What is useful information for my project?'

Make sure you use the information you have gathered to help you make decisions about your designs.

Remember – sometimes you have to make decisions not just from what you have found out but also from what you feel.

Generating ideas

In this section you will find some help in producing a range of first ideas. You should always produce several – there is always a number of different ways to achieve what you want to.

Designing by yourself is very difficult – it is often better to work with others or to use existing products to give you starting points. You can use fantasy too to help your creativity.

Designing and making has improved people's lives in millions of ways. Being creative is one of our most precious abilities. All the works of art that surround us, all the products on which our lifestyles depend, come from original ideas. Some ideas are original combinations of existing ones or are developments from them.

Being creative is deeply satisfying, and fun (though people's ideas can also be harmful).

How do we start to generate ideas? To help you, here are some ways to start you thinking about your design tasks creatively.

Using other people

Brainstorming

You may have tried brainstorming ideas. This is used by professional designers for some very serious work.

These rules will make sure that your brainstorming is as useful as possible:

◆ Choose one person to take notes (this needs to be someone who can write fast).
◆ Agree not to make fun of anyone's ideas – no criticism allowed.
◆ Nothing is too silly to be suggested.
◆ Wild ideas are welcome.
◆ Add to each other's ideas.
◆ Set a time limit (say five minutes).

Now try to get as many ideas down as possible in the time allowed.

◆ Always listen to what others say.
◆ See how you can add to their ideas.
◆ Try to give as many ideas as others.
◆ Make sure your ideas get recorded.

You can record your ideas in a spider diagram. After the brainstorming session you can look at each idea more carefully.

Consultations

Another way you can get help with ideas is to start on your own then call on a friend or two. Designers never think of it as cheating. In the end the ideas will be yours, because you will have to develop them further, and make sure they are original, at least in some ways.

Once you have started a spider diagram, or a bubble chart, ask others to add some legs to it. Then make it yours again by adding to their ideas.

①

②

③

Group crits

Advanced students of design in places like the Royal College of Art often sit down together when they are part way through a project and 'crit' (criticise helpfully) each other's work. Professional designers also do this frequently.

You must prepare for a 'crit' by

◆ making sure your work is all gathered together

◆ getting it sorted into order
◆ making sure others can understand it
◆ making sure your best ideas are shown very clearly (do you need an extra drawing or two – or a summary list to make your ideas clear?).

Then each person starts by saying

◆ what they are working on
◆ why it is like it is
◆ what they are pleased about in their design
◆ and what worries they have.

Each person in the group tries to give positive comments but also criticises what they see as weaknesses in the designing (remembering that everyone else will be doing the same to them!).

Using fantasy to generate ideas

What can you do when you are stuck for ideas? Here are some ways to help you get some ideas started. You can develop the forms you get from them to see if they can become worthwhile products.

Transformations

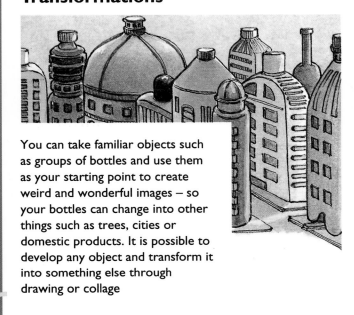

You can take familiar objects such as groups of bottles and use them as your starting point to create weird and wonderful images – so your bottles can change into other things such as trees, cities or domestic products. It is possible to develop any object and transform it into something else through drawing or collage

Changing the size of everyday objects

By changing the size of familiar objects you can produce exciting images in which these objects become something new. Teddy bears can become skyscrapers and toothbrushes become monuments when you make them bigger than their surroundings

By paste up

Using a collage you can paste together fantasy ideas to help you develop new designs. You can put unlikely objects together, such as a landscape pouring out of a teapot, a fish turning into a shell, or these bathroom packages to make a rocket ship

Turning objects inside out

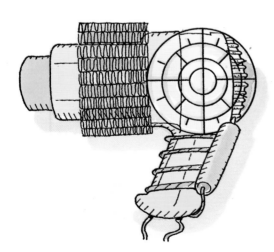

By turning objects inside out you can create new products with futuristic looks. This hairdryer has its internal parts placed on the outside – so a new look is created

Surrealism as a starting point

Look at some of the work done by Surrealists like Salvador Dali or René Magritte. See whether you can develop ideas from dream images

Mixing themes – a Second World War aircraft and a hairdryer

You can mix together two different ideas – often you will come up with a far more creative idea. See how this hairdryer hood came from the front of the aircraft.

Looking at existing products

Identifying design attributes

Designers need to know about customers' needs and their likes and dislikes. This section is to help you to examine existing products as a start to designing something of your own.

When you buy a product you evaluate which aspects of it (**design attributes**) are important to you. Together with the price, this helps you decide which product is the best for you.

We buy products because we need or like them. To help us choose which one to buy, we often compare one product with another. We compare the colour, the shape, the safety features, and the price.

To design a product which is better than the ones we can already buy we need to identify which attributes are important.

We could take any product as an example. Let's try mountain bikes.

Look at the bike in the picture. Make a list of all the important design attributes that you would expect to find on a good bike. Think about all bikes, not just mountain bikes.

Make a chart like the one above and fill it in. Give reasons why the attributes you list are essential for a bike which is well designed.

PRODUCT : BICYCLES

DESIGN FEATURE	Reason why this feature is important.
A comfortable saddle	A rider needs to be protected from bumpy surfaces. It needs to be comfortable for long rides.
Long lasting tyres	

(It will be easier to do this if you look at some real bikes.)

This list might be a good starting point if you wanted to design a new bike. It is a **check list** showing all of the things you need to think about.

Now you know the attributes of a good bike, but bikes are designed for different uses. Look at the following three examples – they have different features for different uses.

Make a list of the special design attributes that each bike needs. You must think carefully about *who* uses each bike and *how* they use it. Comparing different products will give you an even more useful list to start your own designing from, and might even spark-off some original ideas. You can also use this list later to check that the products you are designing have all the attributes the user will want.

Design attributes – conclusion

◆ All products have special attributes.
◆ As buyers we identify the attributes so we know which to buy.
◆ When designing we can start by looking closely at similar products.
◆ Doing this helps us to get a better result.
◆ When you are in the middle of designing you can use your list of attributes to check against.

Designing skills:
Evaluating other products 120

Whatever method you use to generate your first ideas, they will need working on to improve them. The next two sections of *Designing skills* guide you in doing this. They help you to model – in two and three dimensions — and help you to think about aspects you should consider when designing.

Designing skills:
Evaluating ideas 121

Evaluating ideas will also help you to ask questions about your first ideas and to develop them into detailed designs.

Developing ideas—Modelling

Modelling is an important part of designing – we have to know what our designs are going to be like before we start making them. Imagine a bridge designer having an idea for a bridge, building it and finding it was too short! Or building it and finding that it was not strong enough to carry the traffic over it!

Designers make models of their ideas. Modelling helps them to think about their ideas, to test and improve them. If they've modelled it well their design is more likely to work when they make the finished version.

There are many different kinds of model, from the very simple to the complex. They can be in two dimensions (**2-D**), or in three (**virtual 3-D**). A designer may use several different kinds of model for different stages of the project.

Drawings are a form of model. They are quick to do, and cheap. You can use drawings to describe a product. Drawings can also show how ideas start, and how they change and improve.

They can also show how the parts of a product might be joined together (**assembled**) either in two dimensions or in three dimensions.

The diagram below is an exploded engineering assembly diagram for a car component

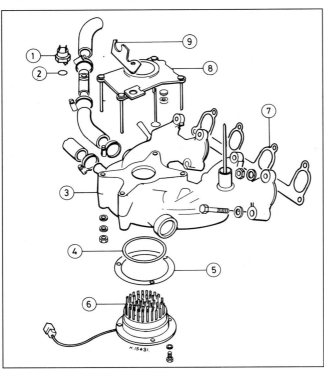

Exploded assembly diagram for a simple shelving unit.

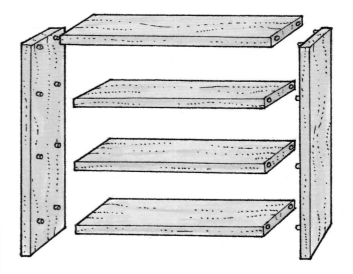

1 Thermo switch for inlet manifold preheating
2 Sealing ring
3 Intake manifold
4 Sealing ring
5 Gasket
6 Intake manifold
7 Gasket
8 Intermediate flange
9 Bracket

Drawings can show how a product might look in its surroundings – for example a new building in a street.

You can use desk top publishing software to present designs for notepaper, posters or other artwork.

You can use other computer-aided design software (CAD) to show designs in both 2-D and virtual 3-D. CAD is used in industry because it can do some amazing things on screen. You can see what your product would look like on the screen by turning it around, stretching it, or making the surface shiny or dull. Or you can look at its parts, and how it is assembled. This type of CAD can drive machines to produce parts directly from the design file (this is called computer-aided manufacture, or CAM).

3-D models and prototypes

Real 3-D models can be useful when you are designing. They can show how the product will work or what it could look like. A 3-D model can show a lot more information than a drawing as you can handle it or walk around it.

It can look exactly like the final product without being like it in any other way.

When a product is to be mass-produced, designers make several models to develop the design closer and closer to the final product. These are called **prototypes**.

A prototype of a car under test

A solid wood and clay **buck** of a car design

Sometimes models called **lash-ups** are used to test if an idea works, even though they may not look like the real thing. Designers use lash-ups to test a mechanism, electronic circuit or other functional aspect of their design.

In school a model or advanced prototype will usually be the end product of your design work. Sometimes though, you might develop your prototypes to produce a batch of products.

Drawing your ideas

Sketches

Sketches can use any drawing technique or system. Be bold and relaxed when you do them but try to make them clear and accurate. Sketch quickly and lightly. Don't worry if you go wrong – get your ideas down as quickly as possible.

Often it is vital to use colour right from the start, either because colour is part of the design or just to pick out parts that make your drawing clearer.

An early design sketch for the Maclaren F1 sports car

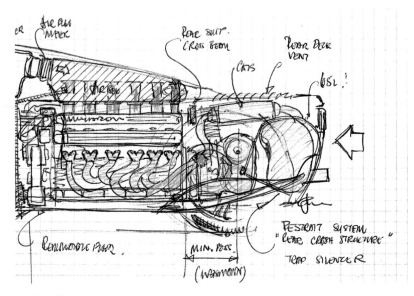

Annotated sketch sheets

There is an old saying: 'A picture speaks a thousand words'. But some things can not be shown by a drawing. Sketches of designs need words as well – notes or **annotations**.

These notes remind you of the thoughts you had as you did the drawing. You might forget some of these points otherwise. You also need them to discuss with your teacher.

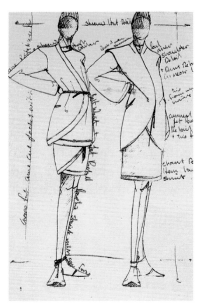

Drawing systems

We show three formal drawing systems three on the next pages. These systems make the drawings very clear.

You may use these systems to sketch your very first ideas, or to develop the ideas into detailed designs. When you need to make drawings more realistic you need to show their colours and textures, which you do by rendering them.

Orthographic Projection

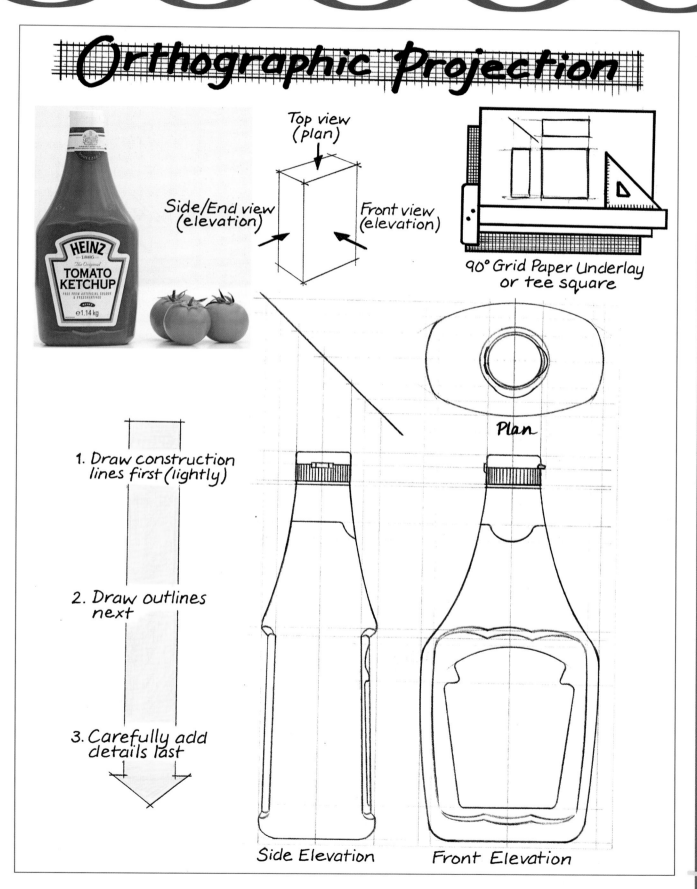

Top view (plan)

Side/End view (elevation)

Front view (elevation)

90° Grid Paper Underlay or tee square

1. Draw construction lines first (lightly)

2. Draw outlines next

3. Carefully add details last

Plan

Side Elevation

Front Elevation

HEINZ
1886
The Original
TOMATO KETCHUP
FREE FROM ARTIFICIAL COLOUR & PRESERVATIVES
e 1.14 kg

Oblique Projection

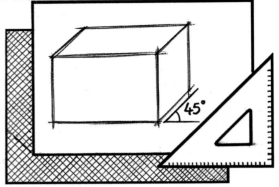

45° Grid Paper Underlay

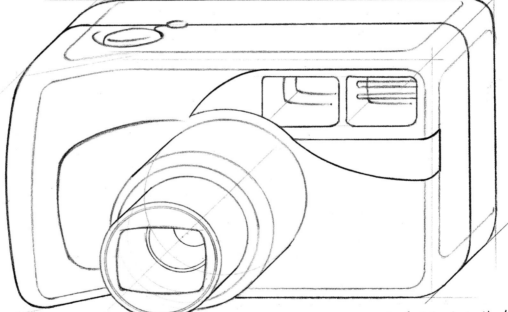

3. Add details last

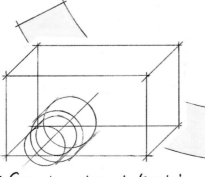

1. Construct main 'crate' first (lightly)

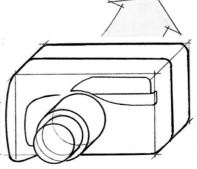

2. Darken important lines next

Isometric Projection

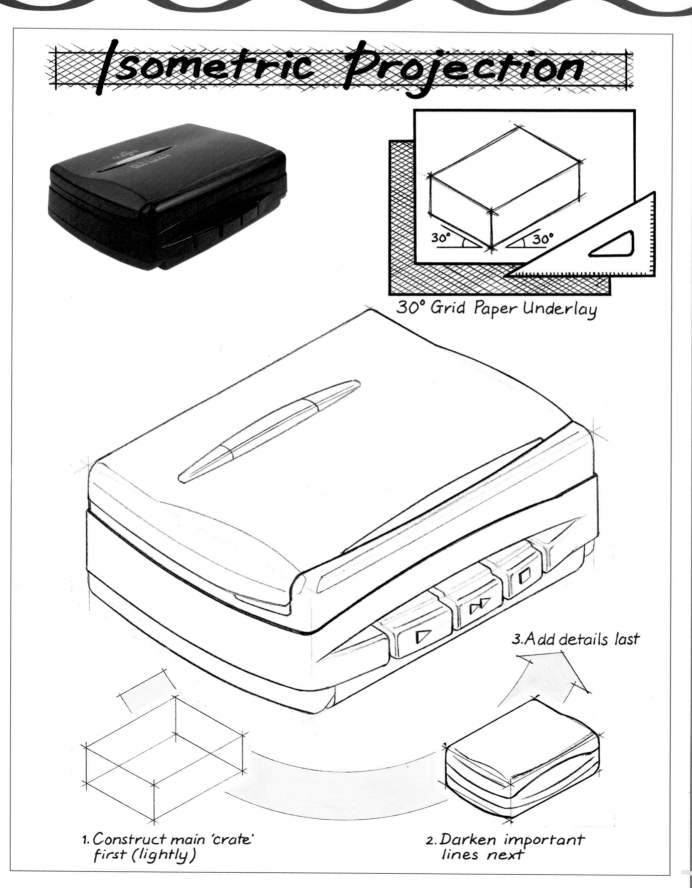

30° Grid Paper Underlay

1. Construct main 'crate'
   first (lightly)

2. Darken important
   lines next

3. Add details last

Rendering in Graphite

Practice Exercises

Three different tones using the same pencil

Darkening the tone by shading in different directions

Hatching-shading lines in one direction, then over the top in another

Fading the tone evenly from light to dark

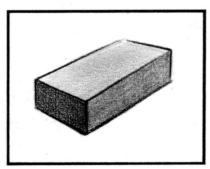

Imagine a light shining on the object – Here from over your right shoulder

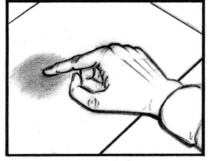

Smudge pencil using your finger to create a smooth, even area of shading

Shade up to a rule if a straight edge is required

Rendering in Colour

Practice Exercises

Three different shades of colour using the same pencil

Darkening the colour by shading in different directions

Fading the colour evenly from light to dark

Fading one colour into another using two or more pencils

HEINZ
TOMATO KETCHUP

1. Start with a clear and accurate line drawing
   - Not necessarily in black

2. Build up colour gradually
   - in layers

3. Continue to add shading
   Carefully add details last

Good drawing relies on accurate observation
Look carefully at objects

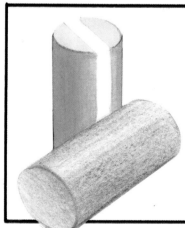

For shiny surface finishes use high contrast between light and dark tones - For dull finishes use less contrast

Rendering light and dark coloured wood using coloured pencils

Modelling food ideas

Testing and costing recipes

For some types of product, drawings are not a very useful way of developing and testing ideas. When you are designing a new food product it's more helpful to note down your thoughts as a recipe than to draw them. Food technologists develop their designs by making small amounts (samples), changing the recipe slightly each time. For example, with a yoghurt recipe they might vary how much fruit they add to each sample. They test them by tasting and by comparing how they look.

Food tasting in a test kitchen with a variety of samples

As well as a food's taste and appearance, its nutritional value may be important. For example, a food technologist who wants to develop a recipe which is lower in fat and sugar can use a computer spreadsheet to show the fat and sugar content of each recipe. They change the ingredients until they develop a recipe which is lower in fat and sugar. They can then make their product and test it on people who are likely to buy or eat it.

Once the product has been tested, the company making it needs to work out how much it will cost, design the packaging, and decide what price to charge for it.

Using numbers to model changes in a design

Designers use spreadsheets to show the costs of producing their product. This is especially useful when it will be produced in **batches**. As the designer changes the amount of any ingredient, the spreadsheet shows how this affects the cost of the product. Costs vary depending on the number of products produced.

DEPARTMENT: BISCUITS

Product Name	Product Code	Unit	Portion Weight	ENERGY kJ	ENERGY kcal	PROTEIN	CARBO HYDRATE	OF WHICH SUGARS	FAT	OF WHICH SATURATES	DIETARY FIBRE	SODIU
DIGESTIVE BISCUITS	00741095	GRM	16.00	2141	510	5.9	66.7	20.8	23.8	10.6	2.6	0.5
HIGH FIBRE DIGESTIVES	00911962	GRM	13.00	2055	489	7.0	62.3	15.1	22.9	10.1	6.2	0.5
MILK CHOC DIGESTIVES	00747004	GRM	12.80	2162	515	6.1	64.7	29.9	25.5	12.6	2.3	0.4
PLAIN CHOC DIGESTIVES	00747103	GRM	12.80	2139	510	5.5	63.9	28.8	25.6	12.7	2.2	0.4
RICH TEA FINGER BISCUITS	00741422	GRM	5.10	1970	466	6.8	75.7	21.3	14.5	6.4	2.3	0.4
RICH TEA BISCUITS	00741316	GRM	9.70	1939	460	6.9	71.6	25.5	15.7	7.1	2.4	0.5
600G RICH TEA BISCUITS	00432184	GRM	9.70	1939	460	6.9	71.6	25.5	15.7	7.1	2.4	0.5
MILK CHOC CRUNCH BISCUIT	00746960	GRM	6.82	2073	493	6.8	65.6	35.5	22.5	10.4	1.2	0.4
ALL BUTTER VIENNESE	00423069	GRM	8.33	2167	518	5.8	63.1	19.6	26.9	16.4	1.7	0.4
COCONUT KISSES BISCUITS	00543606	GRM	8.33	2125	509	6.4	54.4	24.9	29.5	20.3	6.4	0.3
GINGER SNAP BISCUITS	00741538	GRM	8.20	1873	445	5.4	76.7	40.9	12.9	5.3	1.5	0.4
CHOCOLATE CHIP COOKIES	00741750	GRM	11.50	2116	506	6.0	62.1	32.3	25.9	13.4	1.2	0.4
500G CHOC CHIP COOKIES	00876100	GRM	11.50	2116	506	6.0	62.1	32.3	25.9	13.4	1.2	0.4

A section of a spreadsheet showing a nutritional analysis of food

3-D modelling in card

Some students are designing a learning toy or piece of **soft sculpture** in textiles. It can also be used as a cushion by partially-sighted children.

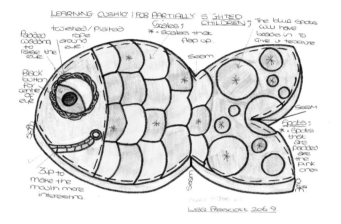

Colour, texture and safety are important. The students draw their ideas, but before they can go on they need to know what their design will look like in 3-D. To do this, they make card models. They can change these simple models until they are happy that the design meets the need. The next step is to make the prototype using the chosen materials and method.

You can use card modelling to experiment with different layouts. Here students are seen cutting out and making shapes which can

later be formed using sheet material (such as sheet acrylic or sheet steel).

Not only is it quick to model in card but it is cheap – you can avoid wasting expensive materials when you are trying out your ideas.

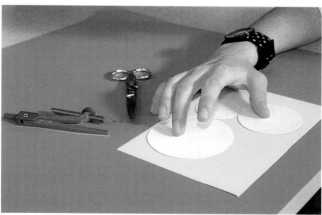

This student is using card to show how **gear mechanisms** might mesh together. It is not a working model but shows the sizes and the spacing needed.

Working with card

First, draw the shapes you want to cut and fold **accurately**. If you do not do this correctly the shapes will not fit together well.

Always check before cutting your shapes.

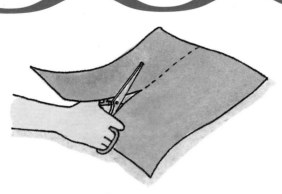

Do *not* use scissors for cutting because they will buckle the card

Use a **safety rule** as a guide when cutting

Use a **craft knife** for straight cuts, especially in thick card

Use a safety rule and a blunt knife or a scissors blade for weakening (**scoring**) the card for a fold

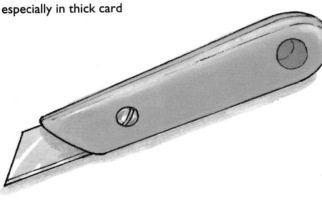

Use a **scalpel** for cutting thin card or curves

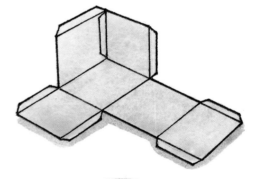

Remember! Leave extra material for **tabs** to glue or slot together

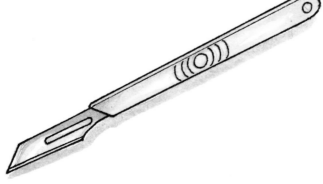

Always cut on a cutting board to prevent damage to the table top and the cutting blade.

3-D modelling with corrugated plastic board

These students are using corrugated plastic board to model A4 document holders for word processor operators. They create full size 'lash-ups' (working models) of their ideas – the hinges move, the bar slides up and down and the stand can be moved to different angles.

The lash-up shows how parts can fit together and work. You can cut plastics board using craft knives. You can make it up quickly and easily too, using a glue gun, plastic rivets and plastic joiners. You also can take it apart easily and alter sizes, shapes and so on, as you change your design before you make your final product using your chosen materials.

3-D modelling with easily-moulded materials

Not all designs can be modelled with stiff materials like card and plastics sheet.

You may need to use soft, easily worked (**malleable**) materials to let you design as you go along. This is like sketching, but in 3-D. The easiest materials to use are clay-like, for example potter's clay, 'Plasticene' and 'Fimo'.

Using a vacuum former for modelling prototypes

The vacuum former is a good way of making items with a high quality finish. These students used their models to test how they looked and how they fitted in the hand (**ergonomics**). The models are prototypes of designs for a computer mouse, vacuum-formed from polystyrene sheets.

To use a vacuum former to make a prototype, first draw some ideas for shapes. Then produce a suitable former (a block to mould the polystyrene over). You can use **MDF (Medium Density Fibreboard)**, pieces of card, or lengths of string and wire. Cut and shape the materials for the former and try different layouts. Finally, paint the shells that have been vacuum-formed, and add bases to complete your models. People who might use the product can then test your models.

Students' vacuum-2 models

Modelling electrical circuits

Electrical circuits can be modelled by drawing, by diagrams or by connecting real components temporarily to make sure the circuits work. You can do this quickly and take the circuit apart afterwards – this is called breadboarding. When designing electronic circuits, electronics kits can be very useful.

Electric buggy challenge 66

You need to experiment and test to make sure you choose the right components for the design. Here, some students are investigating how a variety of components work together.

This is a model of a circuit for a baby alarm. The students are investigating how sound (such as the baby crying) can activate an alarm and produce an output that we can see or hear (such as a flashing light or alarm buzzer).

Developing ideas— things to think about

Thinking about production

The quicker and easier it is to make something, the more you can make, and the cheaper each one becomes.

◆ It takes one hour for a cook to make and bake a loaf. This is called **one-off production**.
◆ If two cooks work together, sharing the tasks, they can make enough mixture for three loaves, and bake them all together in the same oven. This is known as **batch production**.
◆ If four cooks organise themselves and their kitchen into a continuous cycle of production, then they can easily make ten loaves an hour. This process is called **mass production**. With special equipment it can become **continuous production**.

When you are designing you should think carefully about the most efficient way to make your product. You may choose a particular material, or decide to develop a certain shape because it will be easier to make.

Another thing to think about is how a group of you might work together to make something more quickly.

◆ Could the production of any of your design ideas be made easier in this way?
◆ Would using a card template make marking out quicker?
◆ Would using a template make you more accurate?

A simple template being used to mark out a complex shape on the sides of a wooden box

Using templates
A designer is developing a **relief** pattern (a pattern that is cut into the wood) on the sides of a rectangular wooden box. Her first idea was to have a different design on five of the faces, but this would mean measuring and marking out five times. To solve the problem she decides to use the same design five times and cut out a card template of the shape to draw round.

Batch production
The designer then looks at how she will prepare the sides of the rectangular box. Her design means she has to make two each of three different sized pieces. There is no reason why the box shouldn't be a cube, so she changes the design as it will be much quicker to cut out six identical pieces. They can all be done in one go.

Shape repeated and identical pieces cut

Waste wood

Cutting layers of wood together
(they would need to be clamped).

◆ Can you save time by making more of your parts the same size?
◆ Could they all be prepared together, rather than one at a time?
◆ For another task you might find that you need to cut out the same shape four times. You could do this more quickly by cutting out the four pieces of material at the same time.

Vacuum-forming a mould for casting

You use moulds to produce things in materials that can be made **fluid** (liquid). One example is jelly, which starts off as a liquid and then sets in a light metal or a plastic mould. Plastics are also injected into moulds to make items like telephones and calculator cases. It is much quicker to produce several parts from one mould than to make each one separately.

A food technologist is creating shapes for new animal-shaped snack-bars. He uses a mould to cast a series of identical, complex shapes. The moulds can also be used to make vacuum-formed plastic packages for the snack-bars.

◆ Could any parts of your design be moulded?
◆ How might this affect the design of the shapes to be moulded?

Making a mould

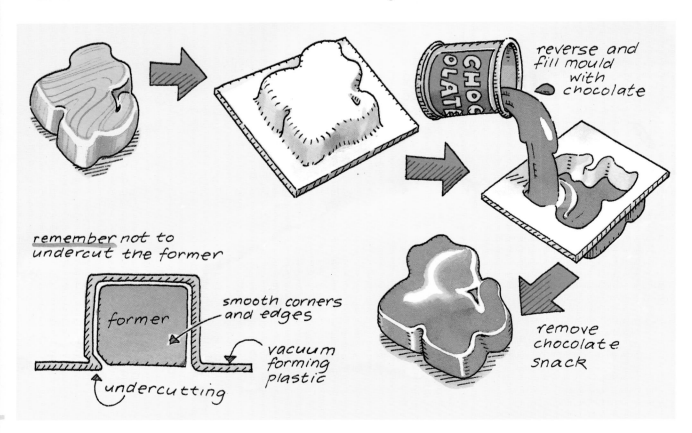

reverse and fill mould with chocolate

remove chocolate snack

remember not to undercut the former

former

smooth corners and edges

vacuum forming plastic

undercutting

Dividing up the labour

A textile designer is asked to make a quilt for a special client at very short notice. There is no way that one person can make up the design in the available time. So instead the designer asks four people to each make square sections. She then joins together the **sub-assemblies** to make a quilt.

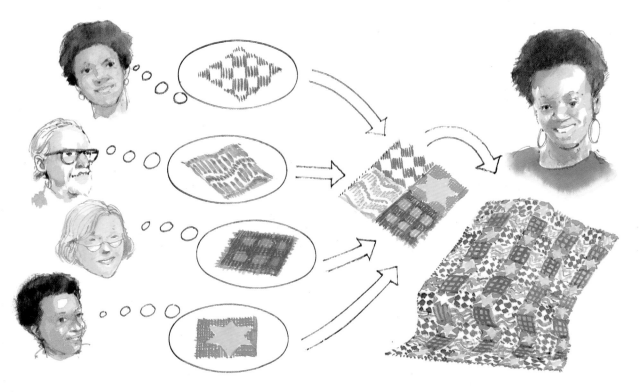

Dividing up the labour

◆ If a group of you is working together on a task could you divide up your labour in a similar way?
◆ Can you think of other ways of dividing up a production process between a number of people?

Suppose you were designing something like a quilt, with 64 identically shaped pieces. Four people could each produce 16 squares and join them to each other. Then they could join these sub-assemblies together to make one big quilt.

Thinking about Aesthetics

To design a product that looks good, feels good and is good in other ways too, you need to think about shape, texture, colour, fashion and culture. These are the **aesthetics** of your design.

Shape

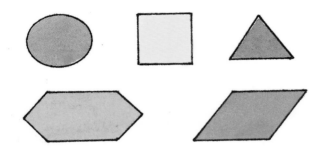

Geometric shapes

Textures

How do you want your design to feel? How will you make it feel that way?

Smooth like glass, shiny metal or smooth plastic?

Rough like sandpaper, breeze block or rock?

Colour

You can use colour for different purposes. Which colours should you use on your design?

Bright colours stand out from the background, are lively and cheerful or may be aggressive.

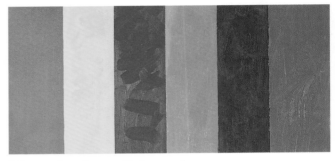

Natural colours link products to nature.

Subdued colours blend into the background and are gentle on the eye.

Expressive colours (or colours with meaning) are colours which establish a mood.

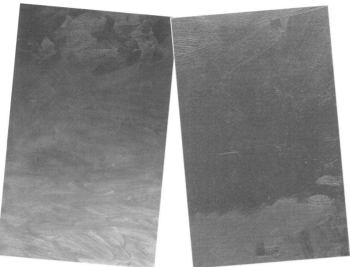

Blue (cold, cool)   Red (warm, exciting)

Harmonious colours go together smoothly.

Contrasting colours are powerful and can be exciting.

Fashion

Is your design up-to-date? – Is it in fashion today?

Or is it old-fashioned? Does it look back to represent a time in history?

◆ Should your design look up-to-date (contemporary)?
◆ What age group are you designing for?
◆ What would suit them?

Culture

Have you thought about cultures other than your own? Would your design appeal to people from your own country? People from a different country?

Other senses

Which of the examples above do we judge with our eyes? The answer is of course, shape, texture, colour and fashion. We have five senses though, and they can all appreciate the aesthetics of a design.

We *feel* texture as well as see it.

We *taste* things. If we like the taste of our food it pleases us aesthetically.

We *hear* things. Have you ever heard a car door crash shut and hated it? If it shuts with a gentle clunk it is more aesthetically pleasing. Some car companies have spent millions to get this right.

We *smell* things. When do you think designers use smell to give us a pleasant aesthetic response? Cupboards give one answer. Some furniture is finished with nice-smelling polish so when we look at it in the shop we feel good – and might buy it.

Thinking about the environment

We are using up the earth's valuable resources. Producing goods has damaged the atmosphere and destroyed the way of life of many cultures and societies across the globe.

Designers have a responsibility to make sure that the products they create will not harm the environment. Remember the three Rs:

◆ *Reduce* the amount of materials being used. Could they be thinner, lighter or smaller in any way? *Reduce* the amount of energy being used.
◆ *Recycle* materials. Can you make the product from materials from recycled products such as glass, paper, aluminium foil or clothes? Will the materials you use be recyclable in their turn?
◆ *Re-use* existing parts. What will happen when the product is thrown away? Can any parts such as motors, fastenings or packaging be used again easily?

We also need to think about how easy it is to maintain our product. Is it easy to repair or replace parts when they go wrong, or do we have to throw the whole product away?

You need to think carefully about designing a product which can be made in an environmentally-friendly way.

Where might pollution cause a problem in the environment ?

Less is more

A puppet theatre company is designing puppets for a new play. They had always used hardwood for their puppets' bodies before but are worried because hardwoods take hundreds of years to grow. They find they can use papier-mâché from recycled paper instead. This is better environmentally, and cheaper and easier, and makes the puppets easier to operate because they are lighter.

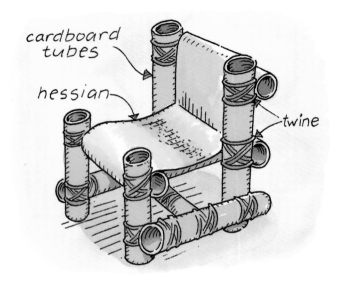

cardboard tubes

hessian

twine

◆ Could your design use less material?
◆ What could be made smaller, lighter or less bulky?
◆ Could you use different, more environmentally-friendly materials to achieve the same result?

Recycled seating

A design company which makes furniture from waste materials is developing ideas for a chair. It develops an attractive idea using thick cardboard tubes from the centre of carpet rolls, bound together with twine. They cover the seat and back in hessian, from old sacks, which they dye an attractive colour. They create a product which is made only from recycled materials.

◆ What waste materials are easily available to you?
◆ Could you use any of them in your designs?

Material matters

A textile manufacturing company is concerned about the pollution it is causing by bleaching and dyeing its materials. It decides to use more **regenerated** (recycled) and **synthetic** (man-made) fibres, and designs better control systems for the waste-products.

◆ Where do your materials come from?
◆ Are there any less environmentally-damaging alternatives?

Biopackages

A packaging company wants to stop using expanded polystyrene, which is environmentally dangerous to manufacture and dispose of. It develops the idea of using paper pouches filled with chopped straw, which can be easily shaped around fragile products. The pouches are easy to re-use and clean to store, and when you throw them away they decompose on a compost heap.

◆ Find out what **biodegradability** is.
◆ How long will your materials continue to exist after they have been thrown away?

Communicating ideas

This is a prompt chart to make you think about how you can communicate your designs:

	Aspect of designing	What you might do	How to do it
1	Examining the context	Visits, videos, descriptions	Discussions, video, audio recordings
2	Generating ideas	Display	Mood boards, style sheets
3	Recording ideas	Sketch plans, elevations, sections	CAD, electrical circuits
4	Market research	Survey	Interview, investigations
5	Analysing the results	Pie charts, bar charts, summary	Star profiles
6	Recording decisions	Annotated diagrams/sketches	List of reasons
7	Developing the ideas	Detailing the product	Sketches, drawings, annotations
8	Testing models	High detail visuals, functional tests	Drawings, models, lash-ups
9	Developing a proposal	Writing up plans, presenting drawings	Writing, annotating drawings
10	Managing time	Scheduling stages	Story boards, GANNT charts
11	Selecting the resources	What can I provide? What's in school?	Investigating, listing, choosing
12	Estimating the costs	Materials, time, overheads	Listing, calculating
13	Planning production	Listing stages, locating materials and equipment	Flow charts, GANNT charts, story boards
14	Quality control	Identify possible problems	Flow chart with check points
15	Meeting the difficulties	Word explosion	Discussion with client, teacher
16	Testing the product	Use it and write report	Client uses and reports
17	Evaluating the product	Check the specification	Check with client, and others
18	Evaluating the process	Flow chart of stages examined	Summary
19	Evaluating your learning	Reflecting, comparing	Writing

You may not know anything about some of the 'How to do it' methods but you will learn about them later in your course.

Remember this chart – it will be useful for you to check against in future years

Planning

This section will help you learn how to plan your designing and making. You need to plan your time and how you will produce your designs.

Planning your time

Good planning helps us to organise our work before we start, so that we know

◆ what we have got to do
◆ when we need to do it
◆ what resources we need
◆ what resources we can use
◆ that we will be ready for the next stage

so we can finish work that we are proud of, within the time allowed.

Learning how to plan

At this stage in your schooling your teacher will probably take charge and help you plan your work. They will probably tell you how long you have got and how much you have to do. As you get older you should be able to make your own plans. By the time you are 16 you should be in charge of your own planning – you will be responsible for your own projects.

This takes practice. You will learn to do it well only if you sometimes try to estimate how long it will take to carry out a task, how much it will cost, and so on. Then you need to see if you were right or why you were wrong.

You are not expected to be responsible for planning all your time at this stage, but you should use one or two Challenges to practise keeping track of how you use time.

Keep a log – or record – of the tasks you need to go through to design and make your product. List them in the order in which you will do them (this is best done on a word-processor).

Put against each task on your list the time needed for them. Plan for lesson time and homework time.

Monitoring and evaluating progress

Once you are making your product it is easy for you to lose track of time.

Check frequently (each lesson?) and add comments to your log:

◆ Have I done enough?
◆ If not, how can I make up?
◆ If I carry on as I am will I run out of time?
◆ How might I do this step quicker in future?

Look back to your task and see if what you are doing is still suitable:

◆ Am I going in the wrong direction?
◆ What other approach might I use?

If you find problems:

◆ Note them.
◆ Try writing (in brief note form) how you might get over them or round them. Is there another way?
◆ When you have solved them, explain how you did it.

Evaluating

◆ If your designs are to suit people, you need to evaluate their needs, and make products which aim to satisfy these needs.

◆ You need to evaluate the ideas you generate so that you know which to develop into fully working designs.

◆ Lastly, you need to evaluate yourself and your progress in designing and making.

What is evaluating?

Evaluating means thinking about something and coming to a view about it – you weigh-up its value. Evaluating is all to do with making matters better. But you might not agree with what I mean by better. And I may not agree with you!

Designers also evaluate other products (designed for similar situations) to see if they can design and make them better.

Because you are a student learning about designing and making, you also need to evaluate your work. You need to evaluate:

Designers evaluate a number of things whilst they are designing and making. For example they have to evaluate a situation to see:

◆ whether there is a need for making things better through designing and making

◆ whether their ideas would make things better.

◆ the products you design and make
◆ how you go about your designing and making
◆ your learning – how well you did, and in what ways.

If you do this well, your work will continue to get

Designing skills:
Working with design briefs   87
and
Looking at existing products   94

Evaluating needs

Before we design and make anything we have to ask some questions – otherwise we might rush in and do the wrong thing.

Designing skills:
Knowing what you really
need to do **86**

Ask questions – identify needs

Asking the right questions will help you to evaluate more effectively. For example you might ask:

What needs can I spot?

◆ my needs?
◆ other people's needs?
◆ future needs?

What can you do about these needs? Think about the possibilities, think about the problems. Which look like the best ways to design and make solutions?

Case study – Product First

Product First is a design consultancy based in London. In one of its projects it identifies an opportunity for a new product which keeps wasps away.

This is how its designers evaluate the needs:

◆ Talking to people and discovering their opinions, likes and dislikes

◆ Establishing the market and evaluating who will use the product and why

◆ Examining existing products, evaluating the competition – what are its strengths, weaknesses?

Designing skills:
Generating ideas **90**

Evaluating other products

What exists already?

◆ Find someone else's design solution to a situation similar to the one you are designing for.
◆ What is this design supposed to do? How well does it do it?
◆ How is it put together?
◆ What is it made from?

◆ Is it well made?
◆ Does it look, feel and taste good?
◆ Does it work well?
◆ Is it easy to use?
◆ Would you buy it?
◆ Is it good value?
◆ Is it safe to use?

Case study – Product First

Product First evaluates the existing market by researching other similar products. Its designers examine each product's qualities (features) carefully, looking for the qualities they want to keep and the features they can improve on.

Product First's designers evaluate the material they have collected. Then they choose some of it to create a mood board (collage) of people who would use the product, existing products, and how and where the new product might be used. They use the mood board to give a background picture to help generate new ideas for the product.

The team analyses the competition, evaluating the strengths and weaknesses of each product

They put together product display boards showing the different designs, textures and finishes already available

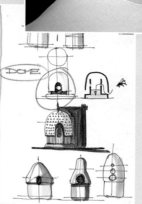

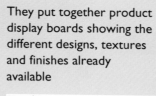

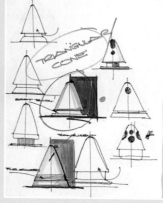

Evaluating ideas

Once you have made a start on your designing and you have thought of several ideas, ask some more questions:

◆ Which ideas do I think are best?
◆ Which are the best aspects of each idea?
◆ Could I combine the best aspects into a new idea?

You can ask some more questions to see if each idea will:

◆ work well
◆ look good
◆ fit in where it will be used

◆ be attractive
◆ meet the needs and opportunities you identified.

BUT – you have to think of your own questions – asking good ones is what starts you on a good design.

Three-dimensional models are useful here to test out the design. They help you evaluate your design before you actually produce it. It's important to spot possible problems and make improvements at this stage. Models can help you do this.

Case study – Product First

The design team begin to sketch ideas, all drawn in rough, in pen (so nothing can be rubbed out and be lost).

They draw as many ideas as possible as quickly as they can.

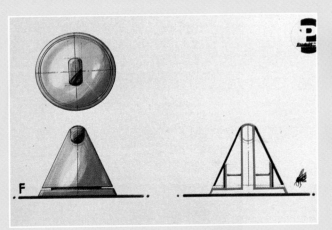

The designers evaluate their ideas. They choose the most interesting ones and work on them in more detail

Final presentation boards allow the designers' clients to evaluate their designs

Evaluating yourself

As you are not only designing, but also learning how to design and learn better, you need to evaluate yourself as well. So you need to evaluate:

◆ your product
◆ your designing and making process
◆ your learning.

Here are some more questions to help you with different parts of this. But remember, you need to think up some questions of your own that are special to what you have done.

Evaluating your product
◆ Did I use the best materials available?
◆ Does it work well?
◆ Does it look, feel, taste, smell and sound good?
◆ Am I pleased with my design?
◆ How well have I made it?
◆ Has it met the needs I identified?
◆ How might I improve it?

Evaluating your designing process
◆ Did you identify the most important needs?
◆ Was your research useful?
◆ How did your research affect your final design?
◆ Did your design change because of what you found out?

Evaluating your learning
Was it easy, OK, or hard to:

◆ find different design alternatives?
◆ gather useful information?
◆ use the materials and equipment?
◆ make your design?

◆ What did you do best?
◆ What do you need to work at?
◆ What advice have you been given?
◆ What is the most useful thing you have learnt?
◆ What will you do differently next time?

Index